I0005157

Raspberry Pi Projects

Building Smart Systems for Everyday Use A hands-on guide to creating DIY projects with Raspberry Pi

THOMPSON CARTER

Table of Content

TABLE OF CONTENTS

Raspberry Pi Projects: Building Smart Systems for Everyday Use 9

What You'll Learn in This Book 10

Why Raspberry Pi? 12

A Hands-On Approach 13

Who Should Read This Book? 14

Building the Future, One Project at a Time 15

Chapter 1 16

Introduction to Raspberry Pi 16

Chapter 2 22

Setting Up Your Raspberry Pi 22

Final Thoughts 26

Chapter 3 28

Understanding the GPIO Pins 28

Chapter 4 35

Programming with Python on Raspberry Pi 35

Chapter 5 43

Building Your First Project: Blinking LED 43

Chapter 6 50

Exploring Sensors and Actuators 50

Chapter 7 58

Working with Displays 58

Chapter 8 66

Creating a Smart Doorbell System..66

Chapter 9...77

Home Automation with Raspberry Pi.......................................77

Chapter 10...86

Smart Temperature Control System..86

Chapter 11...95

Raspberry Pi for IoT Projects...95

Chapter 12...106

Networking and Connectivity..106

Chapter 13...117

Raspberry Pi Camera Projects...117

Chapter 14...126

Smart Lighting System...126

    Step 1: Wiring the Components......................................127

    Step 3: Writing the Code for the Smart Lighting System 129

    Step 4: Running the System...133

    Step 5: Integrating with Cloud Services for Remote Control

   133

    Final Thoughts...135

Chapter 15...136

Building a Smart Mirror..136

    Step 1: Materials Needed...137

    Step 2: Assembling the Physical Smart Mirror...............137

    Step 3: Setting Up the Raspberry Pi and Installing
MagicMirror Software...138

    Step 4: Configuring MagicMirror to Display Information

   140

Step 5: Starting the Magic Mirror 143

Step 6: Customizing Your Smart Mirror......................... 144

Final Thoughts 145

Chapter 16.. 146

Security Systems with Raspberry Pi 146

Step 1: Setting Up the Hardware.................................... 147

Step 2: Writing the Security System Code...................... 149

Step 3: Running the Security System.............................. 153

Step 4: Expanding the Security System 154

Final Thoughts 155

Chapter 17.. 156

Voice-Activated Control Systems.. 156

Step 1: Setting Up Google Assistant on Raspberry Pi 157

Step 2: Setting Up Amazon Alexa on Raspberry Pi 159

Step 3: Creating a Voice-Activated Home Automation
System.. 162

Step 4: Expanding Your Voice-Activated System........... 165

Final Thoughts 166

Chapter 18.. 167

Raspberry Pi as a Media Center... 167

Step 1: Setting Up Kodi on Raspberry Pi 168

Step 2: Setting Up Plex on Raspberry Pi 170

Step 3: Streaming Movies and Music with Raspberry Pi. 173

Step 4: Enhancing the Media Center Experience............. 174

Final Thoughts 175

Chapter 19.. 176

Creating a Personal Web Server 176

Step 1: Choosing a Web Server: Apache vs. Nginx.........176

Step 2: Setting Up Apache Web Server on Raspberry Pi 177

Step 3: Setting Up Nginx Web Server (Alternative Option) 183

Step 4: Accessing Your Personal Web Server Remotely. 185

Final Thoughts 187

Chapter 20...188

Building a Weather Station..188

Step 1: Gathering the Necessary Components.................188

Step 2: Wiring the Sensors to the Raspberry Pi..............189

Step 3: Installing Required Libraries 190

Step 4: Writing the Python Code to Collect Data 191

Step 5: Creating the Web Interface (HTML Template)...194

Step 6: Running the Weather Station 196

Step 7: Accessing the Weather Station Remotely...........197

Final Thoughts 197

Chapter 21...199

Smart Garage Door Opener 199

Step 1: Components Needed...199

Step 2: Wiring the Relay and Sensors.............................200

Step 3: Setting Up Remote Control Using Bluetooth or Wi-Fi..202

Step 4: Adding Security Features.....................................207

Final Thoughts 208

Chapter 22...210

Raspberry Pi for Gaming 210

Step 1: Installing RetroPie on Raspberry Pi...................210

Step 2: Configuring Controllers 211

Step 3: Installing Emulators 213

Step 4: Adding ROMs (Games) 213

Step 5: Playing Games on Your Raspberry Pi 215

Step 6: Expanding Your Gaming Experience 216

Final Thoughts 217

Chapter 23 219

Smart Gardening System 219

Step 1: Components Needed 219

Step 2: Wiring the Sensors and Watering System 220

Step 3: Writing the Python Code to Monitor and Control the
System...222

Step 4: Creating the Web Interface (HTML Template) ...227

Step 5: Running the Smart Gardening System.................229

Step 6: Expanding Your Smart Gardening System..........230

Final Thoughts 230

Chapter 24 232

Raspberry Pi and AI..232

Step 1: Understanding AI and Machine Learning on
Raspberry Pi...232

Step 2: Setting Up the Raspberry Pi for AI Projects........234

Step 3: Setting Up a Basic Facial Recognition System....235

Step 4: Expanding the System 241

Final Thoughts 242

Chapter 25 243

Raspberry Pi for Education..243

Step 1: Why Raspberry Pi is Perfect for Education 243

Step 2: Using Raspberry Pi in Schools and Workshops ..244

Step 3: Teaching Robotics with Raspberry Pi.................248

Step 4: Incorporating Raspberry Pi into Classroom Learning
....250

Step 5: Setting Up Raspberry Pi-Based Workshops 251

Final Thoughts 253

Chapter 26...254

Troubleshooting and Maintenance...254

Step 1: Common Troubleshooting Tips 254

Step 2: Maintaining Your Raspberry Pi 259

Step 3: Ensuring Long-Term Reliability for Your Projects
....262

Final Thoughts 264

Chapter 27...266

Future of Raspberry Pi Projects 266

Step 1: New and Upcoming Raspberry Pi Models...........266

Step 2: How to Keep Up with Emerging Technology and
Continue Building Innovative Projects 271

Final Thoughts 274

Introduction

Raspberry Pi Projects: Building Smart Systems for Everyday Use

The **Raspberry Pi** has revolutionized the world of technology by providing an affordable, compact, and highly versatile computing platform that empowers individuals and organizations to create innovative solutions across a wide array of industries. Since its inception in 2012, the Raspberry Pi has evolved into a powerhouse for DIY enthusiasts, educators, hobbyists, and even professionals. With the ability to support a multitude of applications — from simple automation projects to advanced artificial intelligence (AI) systems — the Raspberry Pi is much more than just a learning tool; it's a gateway to endless possibilities.

In *Raspberry Pi Projects: Building Smart Systems for Everyday Use*, we dive deep into the exciting and transformative potential of this incredible device. This book is designed to provide you with practical, hands-on knowledge for building a wide variety of projects that can make your everyday life smarter, more efficient, and more connected. Whether you're an absolute beginner eager to get started with your first Raspberry Pi project, or an experienced maker looking to take your skills to the next level, this book is your comprehensive guide to creating intelligent systems for the modern world.

The beauty of the Raspberry Pi lies in its simplicity and adaptability. With its tiny footprint, low power consumption, and immense computational capabilities, it can be deployed in a variety of projects that span home automation, robotics, environmental monitoring, educational tools, and much more. Through the chapters of this book, we will guide you through creating systems that not only interact with the physical world but also help improve the way we live by automating tasks and providing real-time insights.

What You'll Learn in This Book

In this book, we focus on **building practical projects** that utilize the Raspberry Pi as the core computing unit, enabling you to develop hands-on skills that are both fun and educational. Each chapter is designed to progressively introduce new concepts and functionalities, so you can master them at your own pace. Here's what you can expect:

- **Getting Started with Raspberry Pi**: We'll begin with a clear, step-by-step introduction to setting up your Raspberry Pi, ensuring you have the tools, knowledge, and confidence to get your device up and running. From installing the operating system to configuring basic settings, you'll get the foundational knowledge needed for all your projects.

- **Building Smart Systems**: As you progress, you'll learn how to build projects that interact with sensors, control devices, and automate systems. Whether it's controlling your home's lighting, creating an interactive science experiment, or setting up an automated irrigation system, the Raspberry Pi will serve as the foundation for turning your ideas into reality.

- **Programming and Software Tools**: We'll dive into Python programming, which is widely used in the Raspberry Pi community for its simplicity and flexibility. Whether you're writing scripts to control hardware or building more advanced machine learning models, you'll learn how to leverage Raspberry Pi's software capabilities to bring your projects to life.

- **Exploring Cutting-Edge Technologies**: From artificial intelligence and machine learning to home automation and robotics, we'll explore some of the most exciting fields that Raspberry Pi is helping to bring to the masses. We'll show you how to integrate AI models, use machine learning for predictive analysis, and control devices through wireless technologies like Bluetooth and Wi-Fi.

- **Troubleshooting and Maintenance**: Ensuring that your Raspberry Pi projects run smoothly in the long term is key to their success. This book includes a section on troubleshooting common issues and maintaining your Raspberry Pi setup for optimal performance and reliability.

- **The Future of Raspberry Pi**: Finally, we'll take a look at the future of Raspberry Pi and its upcoming models, so you can stay ahead of the curve and continue to build innovative, future-proof projects. Whether it's for home automation, education, or industrial use, Raspberry Pi will continue to evolve and open new doors for creators around the world.

Why Raspberry Pi?

With its open-source nature, active community, and massive support ecosystem, the **Raspberry Pi** is more than just a hobbyist tool—it is a gateway to practical, real-world applications. Whether you're a student, educator, engineer, or simply someone interested in learning new technologies, the Raspberry Pi provides a hands-on way to explore the world of computing, hardware interfacing, and software development.

The affordability and accessibility of the Raspberry Pi make it a perfect platform for experimentation. Instead of just reading about theory, you'll have the opportunity to design, build, and test projects that work in the real world. This tactile experience of interacting with the hardware and seeing the results immediately is what makes the Raspberry Pi such a powerful educational tool.

A Hands-On Approach

This book is structured to guide you through practical, real-world projects, making sure that each chapter builds upon the last. Each project has been chosen not only for its educational value but also for its ability to demonstrate how Raspberry Pi can be used to create useful, functional devices that fit seamlessly into your everyday life.

As you work through the projects, you'll get the opportunity to:

- Experiment with sensors and actuators to monitor and control your environment.
- Program and automate devices to perform tasks on their own.
- Build systems that integrate with the web, enabling you to control devices remotely.
- Develop your own custom solutions to real-world problems.

Who Should Read This Book?

This book is for anyone who is curious about the potential of Raspberry Pi and wants to start building practical projects. Whether you're a **beginner** who has just started using Raspberry Pi or an **experienced maker** looking for inspiration, this book offers a wide range of projects and tutorials that will help you hone your skills and make the most of the Raspberry Pi platform.

If you are a **student or educator**, this book can also serve as a comprehensive resource for learning programming, electronics, and computer science concepts through hands-on learning. The projects in this book are designed to be accessible for all levels, ensuring that you can build real-world systems that are both fun and educational.

Building the Future, One Project at a Time

The possibilities with Raspberry Pi are virtually limitless. With each new model, more features are added, allowing you to build even more complex and sophisticated projects. From AI-powered systems to robotics, from home automation to educational tools, the Raspberry Pi is the ideal platform for pushing the boundaries of what's possible in the world of DIY electronics and computing.

In this book, you'll not only learn how to create functional projects, but you'll also gain the confidence to think creatively and explore new possibilities for your Raspberry Pi. The journey ahead will open doors to new knowledge, new ideas, and a new way of thinking about technology.

So, let's get started! With the **Raspberry Pi** at your fingertips, the world of computing and innovation is yours to explore. Through these projects, you'll gain practical experience and, more importantly, learn to think like an inventor—ready to build the future.

CHAPTER 1

INTRODUCTION TO RASPBERRY PI

Overview of Raspberry Pi, Its History, and Its Potential

The **Raspberry Pi** is a small, affordable, and highly versatile computer designed to teach programming and electronics. Originally conceived as an educational tool to inspire and teach young people about computing, it has grown into a powerful platform for DIY projects, prototyping, and even commercial applications. Created by the **Raspberry Pi Foundation** in 2012, the Pi was initially a response to the growing demand for a low-cost computer for schools and hobbyists. It has since become a staple in the maker community, with a global following.

What makes the Raspberry Pi so compelling is its **affordability** and the **vast potential** it offers. With its small form factor, it can be used for a wide range of projects, from building simple electronics to complex home automation systems, robotics, media centers, and even AI applications. Its open-source nature allows users to adapt it to countless creative ideas, making it a perfect starting point for those looking to explore the world of technology.

Different Raspberry Pi Models and Their Specifications

Since its introduction, the Raspberry Pi has gone through several iterations, each offering improvements in performance, connectivity, and capabilities. Here's a look at some of the most popular models and their key specifications:

1. **Raspberry Pi 1 Model B**:
    o CPU: 700 MHz ARM1176JZF-S single-core
    o RAM: 256 MB (later upgraded to 512 MB)
    o Ports: 2 USB 2.0, 1 Ethernet, HDMI, GPIO pins
    o Storage: SD card slot
    o Purpose: Great for basic educational projects and learning programming.

2. **Raspberry Pi 2 Model B**:
    o CPU: 900 MHz Quad-core ARM Cortex-A7
    o RAM: 1 GB
    o Ports: 4 USB 2.0, 1 Ethernet, HDMI, GPIO pins
    o Storage: MicroSD card slot
    o Purpose: Improved performance over the Pi 1, suitable for more advanced projects.

3. **Raspberry Pi 3 Model B**:

- o CPU: 1.2 GHz Quad-core ARM Cortex-A53
- o RAM: 1 GB
- o Ports: 4 USB 2.0, 1 Ethernet, HDMI, GPIO pins, Wi-Fi, Bluetooth
- o Storage: MicroSD card slot
- o Purpose: Powerful enough for projects requiring wireless connectivity like smart home systems.

4. **Raspberry Pi 4 Model B**:
   - o CPU: 1.5 GHz Quad-core ARM Cortex-A72
   - o RAM: 2 GB, 4 GB, or 8 GB options
   - o Ports: 2 USB 3.0, 2 USB 2.0, 2 HDMI, Gigabit Ethernet, GPIO pins, Wi-Fi, Bluetooth
   - o Storage: MicroSD card slot, USB 3.0 for external storage
   - o Purpose: High performance, supports 4K display, and ideal for tasks like web browsing, gaming, and even server applications.

5. **Raspberry Pi Zero / Zero W**:
   - o CPU: 1 GHz ARM1176JZF-S single-core
   - o RAM: 512 MB
   - o Ports: 1 USB 2.0, mini HDMI, GPIO pins (without Ethernet)
   - o Storage: MicroSD card slot
   - o Purpose: A tiny, cost-effective option for compact projects, IoT applications, and portable devices.

Each model comes with **GPIO pins** that allow for easy integration with external sensors, actuators, and other hardware, giving you the flexibility to build a wide range of systems.

How to Get Started with Raspberry Pi

Getting started with the Raspberry Pi is easier than you might think. Here's a basic guide to setting up your first Raspberry Pi:

1. **Choose a Raspberry Pi Model**: Decide which model suits your needs. The Raspberry Pi 4 is the most powerful, but if you're just starting or working on smaller projects, the Pi Zero might be a great budget-friendly option.

2. **Gather the Required Components**:
   o   Raspberry Pi board
   o   MicroSD card (at least 8 GB recommended)
   o   Power supply (5V, 3A for Raspberry Pi 4)
   o   HDMI cable (for connecting to a monitor)
   o   USB keyboard and mouse
   o   Internet connection (Ethernet or Wi-Fi, depending on the model)

3. **Download and Install the Operating System**:

- o The Raspberry Pi runs on **Raspberry Pi OS** (previously known as Raspbian). You can download it from the official Raspberry Pi website and install it using a tool called **Raspberry Pi Imager**.
- o You can also use other operating systems, such as Ubuntu, or even run a media center OS like OSMC or LibreELEC.

4. **Set Up Your Raspberry Pi**:

- o Insert the microSD card into your Raspberry Pi and power it up.
- o Follow the on-screen instructions to complete the setup, including configuring Wi-Fi (if applicable) and setting your locale.
- o You can use a monitor and keyboard directly or access the Pi remotely via **SSH** for headless operation (without a monitor).

5. **Start Exploring**:

- o Once you're up and running, you can start exploring the Pi's potential. Begin with basic programming in **Python**, explore GPIO pin functions, and work through tutorials to build simple electronics projects.
- o You can also use your Pi as a web server, media center, or even a home automation hub—each of which can be expanded as your skills grow.

The Raspberry Pi offers endless possibilities, whether you're learning to program, building a smart home, or creating a personalized project. With its low cost and easy setup, it's the perfect entry point for anyone interested in technology and electronics.

CHAPTER 2

SETTING UP YOUR RASPBERRY PI

A Step-by-Step Guide to Setting Up the Raspberry Pi

Setting up your Raspberry Pi is simple and straightforward. This chapter will walk you through all the steps needed to get your Raspberry Pi up and running.

Step 1: Gather Your Materials Before you start, make sure you have all the necessary components:

- **Raspberry Pi board** (any model you've chosen)
- **MicroSD card** (at least 8GB capacity, Class 10 recommended)
- **Power supply** (5V, 3A for Raspberry Pi 4)
- **HDMI cable** (for connecting to a monitor)
- **USB keyboard and mouse**
- **Monitor** (HDMI-compatible)
- **Internet connection** (Ethernet or Wi-Fi depending on the model)

Step 2: Prepare the MicroSD Card To begin, you'll need to load an operating system onto the microSD card. Here's how:

1. Download the **Raspberry Pi OS** (previously called Raspbian) from the official Raspberry Pi website. The most common version is the **Raspberry Pi OS with desktop**, which is perfect for beginners.
2. Use the **Raspberry Pi Imager** (available on the Raspberry Pi website) to write the operating system to your microSD card.
   o Insert the microSD card into your computer.
   o Open the Raspberry Pi Imager, select the Raspberry Pi OS, and choose the microSD card as the target.
   o Click "Write" and wait for the process to complete. This may take a few minutes.

Step 3: Insert the MicroSD Card and Power Up

1. Insert the microSD card into the microSD card slot on the Raspberry Pi.
2. Connect your **HDMI cable** to both the Raspberry Pi and your monitor.
3. Plug in your **USB keyboard and mouse** to the available USB ports on the Raspberry Pi.

4. Attach the **power supply** to the Raspberry Pi's power port. This will automatically power it on.

The Raspberry Pi will begin to boot up, and you should see the Raspberry Pi logo on the screen.

Installing the Raspberry Pi OS and Connecting Peripherals

Step 4: Initial Setup of Raspberry Pi OS After the Raspberry Pi boots up, the **Raspberry Pi OS setup wizard** will launch to help you configure the system:

1. **Language and Locale**: You'll be asked to select your language, country, and time zone. This ensures that your system uses the correct keyboard layout and time settings.
2. **Wi-Fi Setup** (if applicable): If you're using a Raspberry Pi model with Wi-Fi, you'll be prompted to connect to a Wi-Fi network. Simply select your network and enter your password. If you're using a wired Ethernet connection, this step will be skipped.
3. **Change Default Password**: You'll be prompted to change the default password for security reasons. Set a strong password to protect your system.
4. **Software Updates**: The setup wizard will check for any available updates for the operating system. It is highly recommended to install all the updates to ensure you have the latest features and security patches.

5. **Set Up VNC (Optional)**: If you prefer to control the Raspberry Pi remotely, you can enable **VNC (Virtual Network Computing)**, which will allow you to access the desktop interface from another computer.

Step 5: Connecting Peripherals Now that the Raspberry Pi OS is up and running, let's look at how to connect additional peripherals:

- **Keyboard and Mouse**: Simply plug in your keyboard and mouse into the USB ports. Raspberry Pi OS should automatically recognize them, and you can start using them right away.

- **Monitor**: Make sure the HDMI cable is securely connected to both your Raspberry Pi and your monitor. Raspberry Pi OS will automatically detect the display.

- **Speakers**: If you need audio, connect your speakers or headphones to the 3.5mm audio jack or via HDMI if using a TV with audio support.

- **Camera**: If you have a **Raspberry Pi Camera Module**, you can connect it using the **CSI camera port**. Be sure to enable the camera module through the Raspberry Pi OS settings by navigating to **Preferences > Raspberry Pi Configuration > Interfaces** and turning on the camera.

Step 6: Configuring Advanced Settings

1. **Expand Filesystem**: By default, the Raspberry Pi OS will use only a portion of your microSD card's capacity. To make use of the entire card, go to **Raspberry Pi Configuration > System** and select **Expand Filesystem**.

2. **Enable SSH**: If you want to access your Raspberry Pi remotely via the command line, enable **SSH** (Secure Shell). This can be done under **Raspberry Pi Configuration > Interfaces > SSH**.

3. **Enable Bluetooth**: If you're using a Raspberry Pi with Bluetooth capabilities, you can connect Bluetooth devices by selecting the Bluetooth icon in the top right corner of the screen.

Step 7: Reboot and Start Exploring Once the setup is complete, you can reboot your Raspberry Pi to apply any changes made during the configuration process. After rebooting, you're ready to explore the full potential of your Raspberry Pi!

Final Thoughts

Setting up your Raspberry Pi is a straightforward process, especially with the official setup wizard that guides you through each step. Once you have your Raspberry Pi up and running, you can start experimenting with a wide variety of projects—from simple electronics experiments to complex automation systems. With its easy-to-use interface and robust support from the Raspberry Pi community, you'll find plenty of resources to help you along the way.

CHAPTER 3

UNDERSTANDING THE GPIO PINS

Introduction to General Purpose Input/Output (GPIO) Pins

The **General Purpose Input/Output (GPIO)** pins on the Raspberry Pi are one of the most important features, making it incredibly versatile for DIY electronics projects. These pins allow you to connect your Raspberry Pi to external devices like sensors, motors, lights, and other hardware. GPIO pins can be configured as either **inputs** or **outputs**, depending on the type of device you want to interface with.

- **Input Pins**: These pins read data from sensors or switches. For example, a temperature sensor or a motion sensor will send data to the Raspberry Pi, which can then be processed.
- **Output Pins**: These pins send signals to external devices, like lighting up an LED, controlling a motor, or triggering a relay.

Each Raspberry Pi model comes with a **set of GPIO pins**. On the Raspberry Pi 4, there are **40 pins**, which include 26 GPIO pins, along with power and ground pins. These pins are typically located on a **40-pin header** on the Raspberry Pi board.

The GPIO pins are controlled using software, primarily through **Python**. Python libraries such as **RPi.GPIO** or **gpiozero** make it easy to interact with the GPIO pins.

Basics of Interfacing Sensors and Actuators

Interfacing Sensors: Sensors are devices that detect environmental conditions (e.g., temperature, motion, light, etc.) and send this data to the Raspberry Pi. For example:

- A **temperature sensor** will send the temperature value to an input GPIO pin, allowing the Raspberry Pi to monitor the temperature.
- A **motion sensor** can send a signal to an input pin when it detects movement, triggering an action.

Interfacing Actuators: Actuators are devices that take action based on signals sent from the Raspberry Pi. Examples include:

- **LEDs**: You can control the brightness or turn them on/off by sending signals to output GPIO pins.

- **Motors**: Motors can be controlled through GPIO pins, allowing the Raspberry Pi to power up a motor for tasks like turning wheels in a robot or opening a door.
- **Relays**: Relays act as switches that control high-power devices (like a fan or light). You can use a GPIO pin to switch them on or off.

For interfacing sensors and actuators, you will often need to connect external components to the Raspberry Pi's GPIO pins. Depending on the voltage and current requirements of the sensor or actuator, you may need additional components such as resistors, transistors, or motor drivers.

Real-World Example: Using a Button to Turn on an LED

One of the simplest and most common projects to start with is using a **button** to control an **LED**. This project teaches you how to interact with both an input (the button) and an output (the LED) using the Raspberry Pi's GPIO pins.

Components Needed:

- 1 Raspberry Pi
- 1 Breadboard
- 1 Push button
- 1 LED
- 1 220-ohm resistor (for the LED)

- 1 10k-ohm resistor (for the button)
- Jumper wires

Wiring the Circuit:

1. **LED**:
   - Connect the **long leg** (anode) of the LED to a GPIO pin (for example, **GPIO17**).
   - Connect the **short leg** (cathode) of the LED to a **220-ohm resistor** and the other end of the resistor to the **ground (GND)** pin on the Raspberry Pi.

2. **Button**:
   - Connect one side of the button to a **GPIO input pin** (e.g., **GPIO18**).
   - Connect the other side of the button to **ground** via a **10k-ohm resistor** (this is a pull-down resistor).

Python Code for Button and LED: Now, let's write the Python code that will make the LED turn on when the button is pressed.

```python
python

import RPi.GPIO as GPIO
import time
```

```
# Set up the GPIO mode
GPIO.setmode(GPIO.BCM)

# Set up the button and LED pins
button_pin = 18
led_pin = 17

# Set up the button pin as an input with a pull-
down resistor
GPIO.setup(button_pin,                    GPIO.IN,
pull_up_down=GPIO.PUD_DOWN)

# Set up the LED pin as an output
GPIO.setup(led_pin, GPIO.OUT)

try:
    while True:
        # Check if the button is pressed
        if GPIO.input(button_pin) == GPIO.HIGH:
            # Turn on the LED
            GPIO.output(led_pin, GPIO.HIGH)
        else:
            # Turn off the LED
            GPIO.output(led_pin, GPIO.LOW)
        time.sleep(0.1)
except KeyboardInterrupt:
    # Clean up GPIO settings on exit
    GPIO.cleanup()
```

Explanation of the Code:

1. The **GPIO.setmode(GPIO.BCM)** command sets the GPIO pin numbering system to **BCM** (Broadcom pin numbers).

2. **GPIO.setup(button_pin,   GPIO.IN, pull_up_down=GPIO.PUD_DOWN)** configures the button pin as an **input** with a **pull-down resistor**, ensuring the input reads **LOW** when the button is not pressed.

3. **GPIO.setup(led_pin, GPIO.OUT)** sets the LED pin as an **output**.

4. The `while True` loop constantly checks the button's state:
   o If the button is pressed, the code sets the LED pin to **HIGH**, turning the LED on.
   o If the button is not pressed, the LED is turned off.

5. The `time.sleep(0.1)` adds a small delay to prevent the loop from running too fast.

Testing the Project:

1. Power up your Raspberry Pi and run the Python script.
2. When you press the button, the LED should light up. When you release the button, the LED should turn off.

This simple project demonstrates how to use both **input** and **output** GPIO pins, giving you the foundation to move on to more advanced Raspberry Pi projects, such as building

33

interactive devices, controlling motors, or even creating home automation systems.

By understanding and experimenting with the GPIO pins, you gain control over how your Raspberry Pi interacts with the physical world, making it a powerful tool for creating custom electronics projects.

CHAPTER 4

PROGRAMMING WITH PYTHON ON RASPBERRY PI

Python Basics and How It's Used for Raspberry Pi Projects

Python is the most commonly used programming language for Raspberry Pi projects. It's user-friendly, versatile, and well-supported by the Raspberry Pi community. Python's simplicity and powerful libraries make it ideal for beginners and experts alike. It allows you to interact with hardware, manage data, and create complex systems with minimal code.

In Python, you can use the **RPi.GPIO** library to control the Raspberry Pi's GPIO pins, read data from sensors, and send commands to actuators. Python also supports libraries like **gpiozero**, **PiCamera**, **smbus** (for I2C devices), and more, making it easy to interface with sensors, motors, and other components.

Key Python Concepts for Raspberry Pi Projects:

- **Variables and Data Types**: In Python, you can store data in variables such as integers, strings, and floats. For example, `temperature = 22.5` stores the temperature value as a float.

- **Control Flow**: Python uses `if`, `else`, `elif` statements to make decisions. These are commonly used when checking sensor values to trigger actions (e.g., if the temperature is above a threshold, turn on a fan).

- **Loops**: Loops (such as `for` and `while`) are essential in Raspberry Pi projects, especially when you need to repeatedly monitor sensor values or execute actions.

- **Functions**: Functions in Python allow you to bundle code into reusable blocks. This is useful when controlling hardware or handling multiple tasks in a project.

Python's **simplicity** and **readability** make it the best choice for beginners looking to develop Raspberry Pi projects, while still being powerful enough for advanced applications.

Setting Up a Development Environment

To get started with Python on your Raspberry Pi, you need to set up the development environment. Fortunately, Raspberry Pi OS comes pre-installed with Python, so you don't need to install it manually. However, you'll need a few tools and libraries to get started with coding and building projects.

Step 1: Check Python Installation

First, check if Python is already installed:

1. Open a terminal window on your Raspberry Pi.
2. Type `python3 --version` to check the version of Python installed. The output should look like `Python 3.x.x`.

Python 3 is the recommended version, and it should already be installed on the Raspberry Pi.

Step 2: Install Essential Libraries

Next, install the libraries you'll need to interact with the GPIO pins and sensors. The **RPi.GPIO** library (for GPIO control) and **gpiozero** (a more beginner-friendly library for controlling GPIO) are commonly used.

1. Open the terminal and type:

```sql
sudo apt-get update
sudo apt-get install python3-rpi.gpio
sudo apt-get install python3-gpiozero
```

Step 3: Install an IDE (Optional)

Although you can write Python code directly in a text editor, using an Integrated Development Environment (IDE) can make your coding process easier by providing features like syntax highlighting and code completion. **Thonny** is the default IDE for Python on Raspberry Pi OS and is simple to use, but you can also use **VSCode** or **PyCharm**.

1. To open Thonny, simply go to **Menu > Programming > Thonny Python IDE**.

Step 4: Test Your Setup

Open a terminal or your Python IDE, and test if you can successfully import the RPi.GPIO or gpiozero library. Try the following in your terminal or Python script:

```python
python
```

```python
import RPi.GPIO as GPIO
from gpiozero import LED
print("Python environment is set up!")
```

If you don't encounter any errors, your environment is ready for Raspberry Pi projects!

Real-World Example: Building a Basic Temperature Monitoring System

In this example, we'll build a simple temperature monitoring system using a **DHT11 temperature and humidity sensor**. The Raspberry Pi will read the temperature data from the sensor and display it on the screen.

Components Needed:

- 1 Raspberry Pi
- 1 DHT11 temperature and humidity sensor
- 1 10k-ohm resistor
- Jumper wires
- Breadboard

Wiring the DHT11 Sensor:

1. **VCC Pin**: Connect the **VCC pin** of the DHT11 to a **3.3V** pin on the Raspberry Pi.
2. **GND Pin**: Connect the **GND pin** of the DHT11 to one of the **ground** (GND) pins on the Raspberry Pi.
3. **Data Pin**: Connect the **data pin** of the DHT11 to a **GPIO pin** on the Raspberry Pi (for example, **GPIO4**).
4. **Pull-up Resistor**: Connect a **10k-ohm resistor** between the **VCC pin** and **data pin** of the DHT11 to ensure proper communication.

Step 1: Install the Adafruit DHT Library

To read data from the DHT11 sensor, we will use the **Adafruit DHT** Python library. You can install it by running:

```
nginx
```

```
sudo pip3 install Adafruit-DHT
```

Step 2: Write the Python Code

Now, let's write the Python code to read the temperature and humidity from the sensor and display it on the screen.

```python
python

import Adafruit_DHT

# Define sensor type and GPIO pin
sensor = Adafruit_DHT.DHT11
pin = 4  # GPIO4

# Read the humidity and temperature from the
DHT11 sensor
humidity,           temperature          =
Adafruit_DHT.read(sensor, pin)

# Check if the reading was successful
if humidity is not None and temperature is not
None:
```

```
    print(f'Temperature:          {temperature}°C
Humidity: {humidity}%')
else:
    print('Failed to get reading. Try again!')
```

Step 3: Run the Code

1. Save the file as `temperature_monitor.py`.
2. Open a terminal window and run the script:

```
nginx
```

```
python3 temperature_monitor.py
```

If everything is set up correctly, you should see output like:

```
yaml
```

```
Temperature: 25°C  Humidity: 60%
```

This simple project allows you to monitor the temperature in real-time. You can further extend it by adding a display, sending the data to the cloud, or triggering actions based on certain temperature thresholds.

Explanation of the Code:

1. The code imports the **Adafruit_DHT** library, which handles communication with the DHT11 sensor.

2. It defines the sensor type as **DHT11** and the GPIO pin to which the data pin is connected (in this case, GPIO4).

3. The `Adafruit_DHT.read()` function reads the temperature and humidity data from the sensor.

4. The `if` statement checks if the data is valid (i.e., it was successfully read), and prints the temperature and humidity values. If the sensor fails to provide data, the script prints an error message.

Final Thoughts

Python is a powerful tool for creating projects with the Raspberry Pi, especially when it comes to interacting with sensors, controlling devices, and processing data. This chapter covered the basics of setting up your development environment and provided a real-world example of how to build a simple temperature monitoring system. By mastering Python and understanding how to interface with sensors and actuators, you'll be able to tackle more complex projects as you continue your journey with Raspberry Pi.

CHAPTER 5

BUILDING YOUR FIRST PROJECT: BLINKING LED

Step-by-Step Tutorial on Creating a Simple Blinking LED Project

One of the most straightforward and satisfying projects to begin with is the **blinking LED** project. This simple project teaches you the basics of connecting an LED to the Raspberry Pi's GPIO pins, writing code to control it, and executing the project.

In this tutorial, we will:

1. Set up the circuit with an LED.
2. Write Python code to blink the LED on and off.
3. Execute the code and observe the result.

Components Needed:

- 1 Raspberry Pi (any model)
- 1 LED (any color)
- 1 220-ohm resistor (to limit the current through the LED)
- Jumper wires

- 1 Breadboard (optional but recommended for easy connections)

Circuit Setup

The LED will be connected to one of the GPIO pins on the Raspberry Pi, and a **220-ohm resistor** will be placed in series with the LED to prevent it from burning out due to excess current.

Steps for Connecting the LED:

1. **Anode (longer leg) of the LED**: Connect this leg to a **GPIO pin** (for example, **GPIO17**). This is the pin that will turn the LED on and off.
2. **Cathode (shorter leg) of the LED**: Connect this leg to one end of the **220-ohm resistor**.
3. **Resistor**: The other end of the resistor should be connected to the **ground (GND)** pin on the Raspberry Pi.
4. If you're using a **breadboard**, place the LED and resistor on the breadboard, making sure they are properly connected with jumper wires to the GPIO pin and ground.

This is a simple circuit where the Raspberry Pi controls the state of the LED (on/off) by sending a high or low signal to the GPIO pin.

Python Code for Blinking the LED

Now, we'll write a simple Python program to blink the LED. We'll use the **RPi.GPIO** library to control the GPIO pins.

Step 1: Set Up the GPIO Pins

1. Import the necessary libraries.
2. Set up the GPIO pin that will be controlling the LED.
3. Configure the pin to output a HIGH signal (LED on) and LOW signal (LED off).

Step 2: Write the Code

Open your terminal or IDE (e.g., Thonny) and create a new Python file (e.g., `blink_led.py`). Then, write the following code:

```python
import RPi.GPIO as GPIO
import time

# Set up the GPIO mode
GPIO.setmode(GPIO.BCM)

# Set up the GPIO pin for the LED
led_pin = 17
```

```
GPIO.setup(led_pin, GPIO.OUT)

try:
    while True:
        # Turn the LED on
        GPIO.output(led_pin, GPIO.HIGH)
        print("LED ON")
        time.sleep(1)   # Keep the LED on for 1
second

        # Turn the LED off
        GPIO.output(led_pin, GPIO.LOW)
        print("LED OFF")
        time.sleep(1)   # Keep the LED off for 1
second

except KeyboardInterrupt:
    # Clean up GPIO settings when the program is
stopped
    GPIO.cleanup()
    print("Program stopped.")
```

Explanation of the Code:

1. **GPIO.setmode(GPIO.BCM)**: This sets the GPIO pin numbering mode to **BCM**, which refers to the Broadcom pin numbers (instead of the physical pin numbers).

2. **GPIO.setup(led_pin, GPIO.OUT)**: This sets the chosen GPIO pin (GPIO17) as an **output**, meaning the Raspberry Pi will control this pin (sending HIGH or LOW signals).

3. **GPIO.output(led_pin, GPIO.HIGH)**: This sends a **HIGH** signal (3.3V) to the pin, which turns the LED on.

4. **GPIO.output(led_pin, GPIO.LOW)**: This sends a **LOW** signal (0V) to the pin, turning the LED off.

5. **time.sleep(1)**: This adds a 1-second delay between turning the LED on and off.

6. **except KeyboardInterrupt**: This allows you to stop the program by pressing **Ctrl + C**. When this happens, it runs the `GPIO.cleanup()` function to reset the GPIO pins to their default state, preventing any issues when running subsequent programs.

Step 3: Running the Code

1. Save the Python script as `blink_led.py`.
2. Open a terminal and navigate to the directory where your script is saved.
3. Run the Python script by typing:

```
nginx
```

```
python3 blink_led.py
```

You should see the LED blink on and off every second, and the terminal will show:

```
vbnet
```

47

```
LED ON
LED OFF
```

Stopping the Program:

- To stop the program and clean up the GPIO settings, simply press **Ctrl + C**. This will terminate the code and execute the `GPIO.cleanup()` function to ensure that the GPIO pins are reset to their default state.

Troubleshooting Tips

- **LED not lighting up?** Check your wiring carefully, especially the direction of the LED (anode to GPIO pin, cathode to ground through the resistor).
- **GPIO pin not working?** Make sure you're using the correct pin (GPIO17 in the code). Double-check that the pin number matches the physical pin on the Raspberry Pi.

Final Thoughts

This simple project demonstrates the core concepts of working with **GPIO pins** on the Raspberry Pi. The skills you've learned here—how to set up a circuit, write Python code to control the GPIO pins, and execute the project—are the foundation for many more complex projects. In the future, you'll be able to build on this knowledge to control motors, sensors, displays, and more.

By completing this blinking LED project, you've successfully learned to interact with hardware and control it using Python. This hands-on experience is essential for building more advanced systems and gadgets with your Raspberry Pi.

CHAPTER 6

EXPLORING SENSORS AND ACTUATORS

Overview of Sensors: Temperature, Motion, Light, and Sound

Sensors are devices that detect changes in the environment and send this data to the Raspberry Pi for processing. By interfacing sensors with the Raspberry Pi, you can gather real-world data to trigger actions, monitor conditions, or control systems. In this chapter, we'll explore some common sensors used with the Raspberry Pi, including temperature, motion, light, and sound sensors.

1. **Temperature Sensors**:
   o **DHT11 / DHT22**: These are popular low-cost sensors used to measure both temperature and humidity. The DHT11 is less accurate but is great for basic projects, while the DHT22 provides more accurate readings and wider ranges.
   o **LM35**: This analog temperature sensor gives a linear output corresponding to the temperature. It requires an analog-to-digital converter (ADC) to be used with the Raspberry Pi.

50

- o **TMP36 / TMP102**: These are digital temperature sensors that communicate over I2C, making them easy to interface with the Raspberry Pi.

2. **Motion Sensors**:
   - o **PIR (Passive Infrared) Sensor**: The PIR sensor detects infrared radiation (heat) emitted by objects, such as human bodies, within its range. This sensor is widely used in motion detection systems for security, lighting, and automation.
   - o **Ultrasonic Sensors**: These sensors are commonly used to measure distance, but they can also detect motion by measuring the time it takes for a sound wave to bounce back after being reflected by an object.

3. **Light Sensors**:
   - o **LDR (Light Dependent Resistor)**: LDRs are resistors whose resistance changes depending on the amount of light falling on them. They can be used for automatic light control or to measure ambient light levels.
   - o **TSL2561 / BH1750**: These are digital light sensors that provide precise measurements of ambient light and are typically used for more advanced projects that need accurate readings.

4. **Sound Sensors**:

o **Microphone Sensors**: These sensors pick up sound signals and convert them into analog voltage levels, which the Raspberry Pi can then read. They can be used in voice-activated systems, sound detection, or noise monitoring applications.

Actuators: Motors, Servos, and Relays

Actuators are devices that take action based on signals received from the Raspberry Pi. While sensors provide input, actuators provide output—allowing you to control motors, lights, fans, and more. Let's explore the most common actuators:

1. **Motors**:
   o **DC Motors**: These motors are widely used for tasks like driving wheels on a robot or powering a fan. The Raspberry Pi can control the motor's speed and direction using motor driver boards (e.g., L298N or L293D).
   o **Stepper Motors**: Unlike DC motors, stepper motors rotate in precise steps, making them useful for projects that require fine control, like CNC machines or camera sliders.
   o **Servo Motors**: Servo motors are used for precise angular movement, often used in robotics and

automation. They are controlled by a PWM (Pulse Width Modulation) signal from the Raspberry Pi.

2. **Relays**:

   o **Relay Modules**: A relay acts as an electronic switch that can control high-power devices like lights, fans, or home appliances. The Raspberry Pi controls the relay via its GPIO pins to turn the connected devices on and off. Relays allow the Raspberry Pi to safely control high-voltage systems, even though it only operates at 3.3V.

   o **Solid-State Relays (SSRs)**: These relays are more durable and efficient than mechanical relays. They are often used in more advanced applications that require frequent switching.

Real-World Example: Setting Up a Motion-Sensing Security Light

In this real-world example, we'll create a motion-sensing security light using a **PIR motion sensor** and a **LED light**. The system will turn on the light when motion is detected and turn it off after a short delay.

Components Needed:

• 1 Raspberry Pi (any model)
• 1 PIR motion sensor

- 1 LED (or a 5V relay if controlling a higher-powered light)
- 1 220-ohm resistor (for the LED)
- Jumper wires
- Breadboard (optional but recommended for easy connections)

Wiring the Circuit:

1. **PIR Motion Sensor**:
   o Connect the **VCC pin** of the PIR sensor to the **5V** pin on the Raspberry Pi.
   o Connect the **GND pin** of the PIR sensor to a **GND pin** on the Raspberry Pi.
   o Connect the **OUT pin** of the PIR sensor to a **GPIO pin** (e.g., **GPIO17**) on the Raspberry Pi.
2. **LED (or Relay for a Light)**:
   o Connect the **long leg (anode)** of the LED to **GPIO18** (or another GPIO pin).
   o Connect the **short leg (cathode)** of the LED to one end of a **220-ohm resistor**.
   o Connect the other end of the resistor to **GND** on the Raspberry Pi.

Alternatively, if you're controlling a higher-power light using a **relay**, connect the relay module's input pin to a GPIO pin (e.g., **GPIO18**), the common (COM) terminal to the light's power input, and the normally open (NO) terminal to the light's power source.

Python Code to Control the Motion-Sensing Light:

```python
import RPi.GPIO as GPIO
import time

# Set up the GPIO mode
GPIO.setmode(GPIO.BCM)

# Define the GPIO pins
motion_sensor_pin = 17  # PIR sensor
led_pin = 18            # LED or relay to control light

# Set up the pins
GPIO.setup(motion_sensor_pin, GPIO.IN)
GPIO.setup(led_pin, GPIO.OUT)

try:
    while True:
        # Check if motion is detected
        if GPIO.input(motion_sensor_pin):
            print("Motion detected! Turning on the light.")
```

```
            GPIO.output(led_pin, GPIO.HIGH)    #
Turn on the light (or activate relay)
            time.sleep(10)  # Keep the light on
for 10 seconds
            GPIO.output(led_pin, GPIO.LOW)    #
Turn off the light
            print("Turning off the light.")
        else:
            print("No motion detected.")


        time.sleep(0.1)


except KeyboardInterrupt:
    print("Program interrupted")
    GPIO.cleanup()  # Clean up GPIO settings when
the program ends
```

Explanation of the Code:

1. **GPIO.setmode(GPIO.BCM)**: This sets the pin numbering mode to **BCM**, which refers to Broadcom pin numbers.

2. **GPIO.setup()**: This configures the **motion sensor pin** as an input and the **LED pin** as an output.

3. The `while True` loop continuously checks the motion sensor:

   o If motion is detected (the sensor's output pin is HIGH), it turns the LED on (or activates the relay to control a light).

- o The light stays on for 10 seconds (`time.sleep(10)`), then turns off (`GPIO.LOW`).
- o If no motion is detected, the code waits and checks again.

4. The program can be stopped using **Ctrl + C**, which will clean up the GPIO pins using `GPIO.cleanup()` to prevent potential issues with subsequent programs.

Final Thoughts

This project combines **sensors** and **actuators** to create a useful real-world application—a motion-sensing security light. You've learned how to use a **PIR motion sensor** to detect motion and trigger a light to turn on, which is an essential building block for security systems and automation projects.

With this knowledge, you can expand the project to include other sensors, like temperature or light sensors, and even integrate the system with a home automation platform to control lights remotely or based on other environmental factors. This chapter provided a foundation for working with both sensors and actuators on the Raspberry Pi, enabling you to create more complex and interactive systems.

CHAPTER 7

WORKING WITH DISPLAYS

Connecting and Working with LCD and OLED Displays

Displays are crucial components in many Raspberry Pi projects, providing a visual interface to interact with sensors, control systems, or even display real-time information. In this chapter, we will explore how to connect and work with **LCD (Liquid Crystal Display)** and **OLED (Organic Light-Emitting Diode)** displays, two of the most common types used with Raspberry Pi.

1. **LCD Displays**:
   - **16x2 LCD Display**: One of the most common types of LCD displays is the **16x2 LCD**, which can show 16 characters per line and has two lines. These displays often use the **HD44780** controller, making them easy to interface with the Raspberry Pi using **I2C** (Inter-Integrated Circuit) or **parallel** communication.
   - **I2C LCD Displays**: Most modern LCD displays use the **I2C** protocol, allowing you to control the display using only two data pins—**SCL** (clock)

and **SDA** (data). This makes wiring simpler and reduces the number of GPIO pins required.

Connections for I2C LCD:

- o **VCC** to **5V** or **3.3V** (depending on your LCD model).
- o **GND** to **Ground**.
- o **SDA** to the Raspberry Pi's **SDA pin** (GPIO 2).
- o **SCL** to the Raspberry Pi's **SCL pin** (GPIO 3).

2. **OLED Displays**:

- o OLED displays are small, low-power, and often used in projects requiring compact displays. These displays have higher contrast and wider viewing angles compared to LCDs.
- o **128x64 OLED Display**: A popular size for small projects, these displays use the **I2C** protocol, similar to I2C LCDs, which simplifies connections and makes them ideal for projects with limited GPIO pins.

Connections for I2C OLED:

- o **VCC** to **3.3V** or **5V** (check your OLED model).
- o **GND** to **Ground**.
- o **SDA** to **GPIO 2 (SDA)**.
- o **SCL** to **GPIO 3 (SCL)**.

In both cases, the displays are controlled using Python libraries like `Adafruit_CharLCD` for LCDs or `Adafruit_SSD1306` for OLEDs.

Example: Displaying Real-Time Sensor Data on a Screen

In this example, we'll use an **OLED display** to show real-time temperature and humidity data from a **DHT22** sensor. The sensor will take readings, and the Raspberry Pi will display the temperature and humidity values on the OLED screen.

Components Needed:

- Raspberry Pi
- 1 DHT22 temperature and humidity sensor
- 1 OLED display (128x64, I2C)
- Jumper wires
- Breadboard (optional)

Wiring the Circuit:

1. **DHT22 Sensor**:
   - **VCC** to **5V** or **3.3V** on Raspberry Pi.
   - **GND** to **Ground**.
   - **Data pin** to **GPIO4** on Raspberry Pi (or another GPIO pin).

2. **OLED Display**:

   o **VCC** to **3.3V** on Raspberry Pi.

   o **GND** to **Ground**.

   o **SDA** to **GPIO2 (SDA)**.

   o **SCL** to **GPIO3 (SCL)**.

Step 1: Install Required Libraries

We need to install the libraries for the **DHT22 sensor** and the **OLED display**. Open a terminal and run:

```bash
sudo pip3 install Adafruit-DHT
sudo apt-get install python3-pip
sudo pip3 install Adafruit-SSD1306
sudo pip3 install RPI.GPIO
```

Step 2: Write the Python Code

Next, we'll write the Python script that reads data from the **DHT22 sensor** and displays the temperature and humidity on the OLED screen.

```python
import Adafruit_DHT
import Adafruit_SSD1306
```

```python
import time
from gpiozero import LED
from time import sleep
from PIL import Image, ImageDraw, ImageFont

# Set up the DHT22 sensor
sensor = Adafruit_DHT.DHT22
pin = 4  # GPIO4 for DHT22 data

# Set up the OLED display
disp = Adafruit_SSD1306.SSD1306_128_64(rst=None)
disp.begin()
disp.clear()
disp.display()

# Create an image object for drawing on the
display
width = disp.width
height = disp.height
image = Image.new('1', (width, height))
draw = ImageDraw.Draw(image)

# Set up the font
font = ImageFont.load_default()

try:
    while True:
        # Read humidity and temperature from
DHT22 sensor
```

```
        humidity,           temperature        =
Adafruit_DHT.read(sensor, pin)


        if humidity is not None and temperature
is not None:
            # Draw text on the display
            draw.rectangle((0,      0,      width,
height), outline=0, fill=0)
            draw.text((0,  0),  'Temp:  {:.1f}
C'.format(temperature), font=font, fill=255)
            draw.text((0, 20), 'Humidity: {:.1f}
%'.format(humidity), font=font, fill=255)
            disp.image(image)
            disp.display()
        else:
            print("Failed to get reading.  Try
again!")


        # Wait for 2 seconds before taking
another reading
        time.sleep(2)


except KeyboardInterrupt:
    print("Program interrupted")
    disp.clear()
    disp.display()
```

Explanation of the Code:

1. **Adafruit_DHT.read(sensor, pin)**: This function reads the humidity and temperature from the DHT22 sensor. If the sensor provides valid data, it is stored in the `humidity` and `temperature` variables.

2. **Adafruit_SSD1306.SSD1306_128_64**: This initializes the OLED display, specifying its resolution (128x64).

3. **Image and ImageDraw**: We use these to create an image in memory and draw text (temperature and humidity) on the display.

4. **draw.rectangle()**: This function clears the screen by drawing a black rectangle.

5. **draw.text()**: This function writes the temperature and humidity values on the screen.

6. **disp.image() and disp.display()**: These functions send the image data to the display and update it.

7. The script runs indefinitely, updating the display every 2 seconds with new sensor readings.

Step 3: Run the Code

1. Save the Python script as `sensor_display.py`.

2. Open a terminal and navigate to the folder where the script is saved.

3. Run the script:

```bash
```

```
python3 sensor_display.py
```

You should now see the temperature and humidity values displayed on the OLED screen. The display will update every 2 seconds, providing real-time information about the sensor's readings.

Final Thoughts

Using displays like **LCDs** and **OLEDs** with your Raspberry Pi is a great way to bring your projects to life by providing immediate feedback. In this chapter, you learned how to connect and use these displays, as well as how to display real-time data such as temperature and humidity readings.

This foundational knowledge will allow you to integrate displays into more advanced Raspberry Pi projects, such as monitoring systems, home automation interfaces, or even creating custom dashboards for your IoT devices. With Python and libraries like **Adafruit_SSD1306** and **Adafruit_DHT**, you can easily expand the scope of your projects and present data in a clear and engaging way.

CHAPTER 8

CREATING A SMART DOORBELL SYSTEM

Building a Doorbell System with a Camera and Sensor

A **smart doorbell** system allows you to see and communicate with visitors at your door, even when you're not home. Using the Raspberry Pi, we can build a simple yet effective smart doorbell system that includes a camera for video streaming and a motion sensor to detect visitors. Additionally, we will integrate the system with a mobile phone or web interface to allow you to view live footage and communicate with visitors remotely.

In this chapter, we will:

1. Set up a **motion sensor** to detect when someone is at the door.
2. Connect a **camera** to capture video or images of visitors.
3. Set up a **web or mobile interface** to interact with the system.

Components Needed:

- Raspberry Pi (any model, but a Raspberry Pi 3 or 4 is recommended)
- 1 **PIR motion sensor** (for motion detection)
- 1 **Raspberry Pi camera module** (for capturing video)
- 1 **Buzzer** (optional, to create a doorbell sound)
- 1 **Relay module** (optional, to trigger a light or other device)
- 1 **Microphone and speaker** (optional, for two-way communication)
- **Jumper wires**
- **Breadboard** (optional for easy connections)
- **Mobile phone** or **web interface** (for accessing the system remotely)

Step 1: Wiring the Components

Wiring the PIR Motion Sensor:

- **VCC** to **5V** or **3.3V** (depending on the sensor model) on the Raspberry Pi.
- **GND** to **Ground**.
- **OUT** to a GPIO pin on the Raspberry Pi (for example, **GPIO17**).

Wiring the Camera Module:

- The **Raspberry Pi camera module** uses a **CSI (Camera Serial Interface)** port, which is different from the GPIO pins. Connect the camera module to the **CSI port** on the Raspberry Pi (usually near the HDMI port).

- Ensure that the ribbon cable is securely attached to both the Raspberry Pi and the camera module.

Optional: Wiring the Buzzer and Relay:

- **Buzzer**: Connect the **positive leg** of the buzzer to a GPIO pin (e.g., **GPIO18**) and the **negative leg** to **Ground**.

- **Relay Module**: If you want to trigger a light or other device when someone presses the doorbell, connect the **IN** pin of the relay module to a GPIO pin (e.g., **GPIO22**), and the relay will control the high-power device.

Step 2: Setting Up the Camera

1. **Enable the Camera**: Open a terminal on your Raspberry Pi and run the following command to enable the camera interface:

```bash

sudo raspi-config
```

68

Navigate to **Interface Options** > **Camera**, and select **Enable**. Reboot the Raspberry Pi for the changes to take effect.

2. **Test the Camera**: To test the camera, use the following command in the terminal:

```bash
```

```bash
raspistill -o test.jpg
```

This command takes a snapshot with the camera and saves it as **test.jpg**. You can check the image to ensure the camera is working.

Step 3: Setting Up the Motion Sensor

1. **Install the RPi.GPIO Library**: To control the GPIO pins, you will need the **RPi.GPIO** library. If it's not already installed, run:

```bash
```

```bash
sudo apt-get install python3-rpi.gpio
```

2. **Write Python Code to Detect Motion**: We'll write a Python script to detect motion from the PIR sensor.

The Raspberry Pi will take a snapshot or start recording video when motion is detected.

```python
python

import RPi.GPIO as GPIO
import time
from picamera import PiCamera

# Set up the GPIO pin
motion_sensor_pin = 17
GPIO.setmode(GPIO.BCM)
GPIO.setup(motion_sensor_pin, GPIO.IN)

# Set up the camera
camera = PiCamera()

def capture_image():
    camera.start_preview()
    time.sleep(2)
    camera.capture('/home/pi/visitor.jpg')
    camera.stop_preview()

try:
    while True:
        # Wait for motion to be detected
        if GPIO.input(motion_sensor_pin):
            print("Motion   detected!   Capturing
image...")
```

```
            capture_image()
            time.sleep(5)   # Delay to prevent
multiple captures in a short time
        else:
            time.sleep(0.1)   # No motion, check
again
except KeyboardInterrupt:
    print("Program interrupted")
    GPIO.cleanup()
```

Explanation of the Code:

1. **GPIO.setup()**: Configures the PIR sensor's GPIO pin as an input.

2. **camera.start_preview()**: Previews the camera feed (optional).

3. **camera.capture()**: Captures an image and saves it to the Raspberry Pi's storage.

4. **GPIO.input(motion_sensor_pin)**: Continuously checks the PIR sensor's status. If motion is detected, it triggers the image capture.

5. **time.sleep()**: Pauses between actions to avoid capturing too many images in a short period.

Step 4: Setting Up a Mobile or Web Interface

For remote access, you can create a **web interface** using **Flask**, a lightweight web framework for Python, or use an app to view the camera feed and interact with the system.

71

Option 1: Web Interface with Flask

1. **Install Flask**: Install Flask to create the web interface:

```bash
bash
```

```bash
sudo pip3 install flask
```

2. **Write the Flask Application**: Create a Python script (e.g., **doorbell_web.py**) for the web interface.

```python
python

from flask import Flask, render_template, Response
import time
from picamera import PiCamera

app = Flask(__name__)

# Set up the camera
camera = PiCamera()

def gen_frames():
    while True:
        # Capture a video frame and encode it as JPEG
        camera.capture('/home/pi/frame.jpg')
```

```
        with open('/home/pi/frame.jpg', 'rb') as
f:
            frame = f.read()
            yield (b'--frame\r\n'
                b'Content-Type:
image/jpeg\r\n\r\n' + frame + b'\r\n\r\n')

@app.route('/')
def index():
    return render_template('index.html')

@app.route('/video_feed')
def video_feed():
    return Response(gen_frames(),
                    mimetype='multipart/x-
mixed-replace; boundary=frame')

if __name__ == '__main__':
    app.run(host='0.0.0.0',          port=5000,
threaded=True)
```

This code creates a Flask web server that streams the camera feed. The `gen_frames()` function continuously captures images and streams them to the browser.

3. **HTML for the Web Interface**: Create an HTML file (e.g., **templates/index.html**) to display the video feed.

```
html
```

73

```
<!DOCTYPE html>
<html lang="en">
<head>
    <meta charset="UTF-8">
    <title>Smart Doorbell</title>
</head>
<body>
    <h1>Smart Doorbell Live Feed</h1>
    <img  src="{{  url_for('video_feed')  }}"
width="640" height="480">
</body>
</html>
```

4. **Run the Web Server**: In the terminal, run the Flask app:

```bash
bash
```

```
python3 doorbell_web.py
```

You can now view the camera feed in a browser by navigating to **http://<RaspberryPi_IP>:5000**.

Option 2: Mobile App Integration

For mobile access, you can either:

74

- Use a **web-based mobile app** by opening the Flask server URL on your mobile browser.
- Build a **native app** using frameworks like **Flutter** or **React Native** to access the video stream and send commands to the Raspberry Pi.

Step 5: Finalizing and Testing the System

- **Test the Motion Detection**: Trigger the motion sensor by walking in front of it, and check if the camera captures an image and sends it to the server.
- **Test the Web Interface**: Access the web interface from a computer or mobile device and verify that the video feed is displayed correctly.
- **Optional**: Set up notifications to alert you when the doorbell is pressed or motion is detected. You can use services like **Twilio** to send SMS or **Pushbullet** for mobile notifications.

Final Thoughts

This smart doorbell system is a great example of integrating **motion detection**, **camera capture**, and **remote access** using the Raspberry Pi. By combining sensors and camera modules with web or mobile interfaces, you've created a system that allows you to monitor and communicate with visitors from anywhere.

You can expand this system by adding features like **two-way audio communication**, **cloud storage** for video recordings, or integrating with existing home automation systems for added functionality. With this foundation, the possibilities for smart home automation are endless.

CHAPTER 9

HOME AUTOMATION WITH RASPBERRY PI

Basics of Home Automation: Controlling Lights, Fans, and More

Home automation refers to the use of technology to control devices within a home automatically. With the Raspberry Pi, you can set up systems that control lights, fans, security systems, thermostats, and other household appliances. Home automation can make your life more convenient, energy-efficient, and secure.

Key components involved in home automation with Raspberry Pi include:

- **Sensors**: These are used to monitor the environment (e.g., motion sensors, temperature sensors, light sensors).
- **Actuators**: These control physical devices such as lights, fans, locks, and blinds.
- **Communication Protocols**: Raspberry Pi can communicate with devices using **GPIO pins**, **Wi-Fi**, **Bluetooth**, or **Zigbee**.
- **Software**: Platforms like **Home Assistant**, **OpenHAB**, and **Node-RED** provide pre-built frameworks for

building automation systems. Alternatively, you can write custom scripts using **Python** to control devices.

In this chapter, we'll focus on the basics of controlling home devices like lights and fans using the **Raspberry Pi** and **Python**. You'll learn how to set up an automated light control system, but the same principles can be applied to other home automation tasks.

Components Needed:

- 1 **Raspberry Pi** (any model)
- 1 **Relay Module** (for controlling high-power devices)
- 1 **LED** or **Light Bulb** (for demonstration)
- 1 **Jumper Wires**
- 1 **Breadboard** (optional but recommended for easy connections)
- 1 **Fan or Light** (if using a real appliance)
- **Python** (for controlling the devices)

Step 1: Setting Up the Relay Module

A **relay** is an electrical switch that allows you to control high-power devices using low-power signals from the Raspberry Pi. Since the Raspberry Pi GPIO pins operate at 3.3V, a relay is required to control devices that operate at higher voltages, such as lights (120V/220V) or fans.

Wiring the Relay Module:

1. **VCC**: Connect the **VCC** pin of the relay module to the **5V** pin of the Raspberry Pi.
2. **GND**: Connect the **GND** pin of the relay to the **Ground** pin of the Raspberry Pi.
3. **IN**: Connect the **IN** pin of the relay module to one of the GPIO pins (e.g., **GPIO17**). This pin will control the relay state.
4. **NO (Normally Open)**: Connect the **NO** terminal to the **live wire** of the light or fan (or use the relay to control the LED for the demonstration).
5. **COM (Common)**: Connect the **COM** terminal to the **live wire** of the power supply.
6. **NC (Normally Closed)**: This is optional; it is used if you want the device to be turned on by default.

Safety Note: When working with high-voltage devices, be extremely careful and ensure that everything is properly insulated and grounded. If you are not comfortable working with high-voltage appliances, consider using a **low-voltage device** like an LED for testing.

Step 2: Writing the Python Code to Control the Relay

With the relay module wired up, the next step is to write Python code that will control the relay. This code will turn the light (or fan) on and off.

1. **Install RPi.GPIO**: If you haven't already installed the **RPi.GPIO** library, run the following command in the terminal:

```bash
sudo apt-get install python3-rpi.gpio
```

2. **Write the Python Script**: Create a Python script (e.g., **automated_light.py**) to control the relay. The script will check for input (such as a button press or a sensor) and turn the light on or off accordingly.

```python
import RPi.GPIO as GPIO
import time

# Set up GPIO pin
relay_pin = 17
GPIO.setmode(GPIO.BCM)
GPIO.setup(relay_pin, GPIO.OUT)
```

80

```python
# Function to turn the light on
def turn_on_light():
    GPIO.output(relay_pin, GPIO.HIGH)   # Relay
ON, light on
    print("Light is ON")


# Function to turn the light off
def turn_off_light():
    GPIO.output(relay_pin, GPIO.LOW)    # Relay
OFF, light off
    print("Light is OFF")


# Main loop
try:
    while True:
        user_input = input("Enter 'on' to turn on
the   light   or   'off'   to   turn   off:
").strip().lower()
        if user_input == "on":
            turn_on_light()
        elif user_input == "off":
            turn_off_light()
        else:
            print("Invalid  input.  Please  enter
'on' or 'off'.")
except KeyboardInterrupt:
    print("Program interrupted")
```

81

```
GPIO.cleanup()    # Clean up GPIO settings on
exit
```

Explanation of the Code:

1. **GPIO.setmode(GPIO.BCM)**: This sets the **BCM pin numbering** system for the Raspberry Pi's GPIO pins.

2. **GPIO.setup(relay_pin, GPIO.OUT)**: This configures **GPIO17** (connected to the relay) as an output.

3. **GPIO.output(relay_pin, GPIO.HIGH)**: This sends a high signal to the relay, turning it on and powering the connected device (light or fan).

4. **GPIO.output(relay_pin, GPIO.LOW)**: This sends a low signal to the relay, turning it off.

5. The `while True` loop waits for user input in the terminal. The user can enter `'on'` to turn the light on or `'off'` to turn it off.

Step 3: Running the Code

1. Save the Python script as **automated_light.py**.

2. Open a terminal and navigate to the directory where the script is saved.

3. Run the script by typing:

```
bash
```

```
python3 automated_light.py
```

You will see a prompt asking you to enter `'on'` or `'off'` to control the light. Entering `'on'` will turn on the light, and entering `'off'` will turn it off.

Step 4: Extending the System for Full Automation

To take it a step further, you can automate this process by using a sensor or timer to control the lights. For example, you can use a **motion sensor** (such as a PIR sensor) to automatically turn on the light when someone enters the room.

Example: Motion-Sensing Light Control:

```python
python

import RPi.GPIO as GPIO
import time

# Set up GPIO pins
motion_sensor_pin = 17
relay_pin = 18
GPIO.setmode(GPIO.BCM)
GPIO.setup(motion_sensor_pin, GPIO.IN)
GPIO.setup(relay_pin, GPIO.OUT)

# Function to turn the light on
def turn_on_light():
```

```python
        GPIO.output(relay_pin, GPIO.HIGH)
        print("Light is ON")


# Function to turn the light off
def turn_off_light():
        GPIO.output(relay_pin, GPIO.LOW)
        print("Light is OFF")


# Main loop
try:
        while True:
                if GPIO.input(motion_sensor_pin):    # If
motion is detected
                        turn_on_light()
                        time.sleep(5)   # Keep the light on
for 5 seconds
                        turn_off_light()
                else:
                        time.sleep(0.1)  # Check again if no
motion is detected
except KeyboardInterrupt:
        print("Program interrupted")
        GPIO.cleanup()
```

In this example, the light will turn on automatically when motion is detected and stay on for 5 seconds before turning off. You can adjust the delay as needed.

Final Thoughts

In this chapter, you've learned the basics of home automation with the Raspberry Pi, including how to control devices such as lights and fans using **relays** and **Python**. You've also seen how to extend this system using sensors, like motion detection, to automate the control of your devices. Home automation with Raspberry Pi opens the door to a wide range of possibilities, from simple light control to more complex systems like automated climate control, security systems, and more.

By combining sensors, relays, and the Raspberry Pi, you can create a fully automated smart home system that enhances comfort, convenience, and energy efficiency.

CHAPTER 10

SMART TEMPERATURE CONTROL SYSTEM

Using a Temperature Sensor and Relay to Control Fans or Heaters

A **smart temperature control system** is a key component of home automation, allowing you to maintain a comfortable living environment by automatically adjusting temperature. With the **Raspberry Pi**, a **temperature sensor**, and a **relay module**, you can create a system that automatically controls fans or heaters based on real-time temperature readings.

In this chapter, we will:

1. Use a **temperature sensor** (such as the **DHT22**) to read the current temperature.
2. Control a **fan or heater** using a **relay module** based on the temperature threshold.
3. Build a **smart thermostat** to automatically adjust the temperature by turning the fan or heater on or off.

Components Needed:

- 1 **Raspberry Pi** (any model)

86

- 1 **DHT22 temperature and humidity sensor**
- 1 **Relay module** (to control the fan or heater)
- 1 **Fan or Heater** (for controlling temperature)
- Jumper wires
- Breadboard (optional for easy connections)
- **Python** (for controlling the system)

Step 1: Wiring the Temperature Sensor and Relay

Wiring the DHT22 Sensor:

1. **VCC** to **5V** (or **3.3V** depending on the model) on the Raspberry Pi.
2. **GND** to **Ground**.
3. **Data pin** to a **GPIO pin** (e.g., **GPIO4**).

Wiring the Relay Module:

1. **VCC** to **5V** on the Raspberry Pi.
2. **GND** to **Ground**.
3. **IN** to a **GPIO pin** (e.g., **GPIO17**). This pin will control the relay to turn the fan or heater on or off.
4. **NO (Normally Open)**: Connect the **NO** terminal to the **live wire** of the fan or heater.
5. **COM (Common)**: Connect the **COM** terminal to the **live wire** of the power supply for the fan or heater.

Safety Note: If you're working with high-voltage appliances like heaters, be extremely careful and ensure everything is properly insulated and grounded. If you're not experienced with high-voltage devices, consider using a **low-voltage device** like a fan for testing.

Step 2: Installing Required Libraries

Before writing the Python code, make sure the necessary libraries are installed for reading data from the DHT22 sensor and controlling the GPIO pins.

1. **Install RPi.GPIO**: If not already installed, run:

```bash
sudo apt-get install python3-rpi.gpio
```

2. **Install Adafruit_DHT** (for the DHT22 sensor):

```bash
sudo pip3 install Adafruit-DHT
```

Step 3: Writing the Python Code for Smart Thermostat

Now, let's write the Python script to read the temperature from the DHT22 sensor and control the fan or heater using the relay.

```python
python

import RPi.GPIO as GPIO
import Adafruit_DHT
import time

# Set up the GPIO pins
relay_pin = 17  # GPIO pin to control the relay
motion_sensor_pin = 4  # GPIO pin for temperature sensor

GPIO.setmode(GPIO.BCM)
GPIO.setup(relay_pin, GPIO.OUT)

# Set up the DHT22 sensor
sensor = Adafruit_DHT.DHT22
pin = 4  # GPIO4 for DHT22 data

# Define the target temperature range for the thermostat
target_temperature_high = 25  # Temperature in Celsius to turn on the fan/heater
```

```
target_temperature_low = 22   # Temperature to
turn off the fan/heater


# Function to control fan or heater based on
temperature
def control_temperature():
    humidity,            temperature           =
Adafruit_DHT.read(sensor, pin)


    if humidity is not None and temperature is
not None:
        print(f"Current           Temperature:
{temperature:.1f}°C")


        if              temperature             >
target_temperature_high: # If it's too hot, turn
on the fan
            GPIO.output(relay_pin, GPIO.HIGH)  #
Turn on the fan
            print("Temperature  is  too  high!
Turning on the fan.")


        elif           temperature             <
target_temperature_low: # If it's too cold, turn
on the heater
            GPIO.output(relay_pin, GPIO.HIGH)  #
Turn on the heater
            print("Temperature  is  too  low!
Turning on the heater.")
```

90

```
        else:
                GPIO.output(relay_pin, GPIO.LOW)   #
Turn off the fan or heater
                print("Temperature is within range.
Turning off the fan/heater.")

    else:
        print("Failed to get reading from the
sensor. Please try again.")

# Main loop to keep the system running
try:
    while True:
        control_temperature()
        time.sleep(10)  # Check every 10 seconds

except KeyboardInterrupt:
    print("Program interrupted")
    GPIO.cleanup()  # Clean up GPIO settings on
exit
```

Explanation of the Code:

1. **GPIO Setup**: The code sets up **GPIO17** to control the relay that switches the fan or heater on and off.

2. **DHT22 Sensor Reading**: The **Adafruit_DHT.read()** function is used to read the temperature and humidity values from the sensor connected to **GPIO4**.

3. **Temperature Control Logic**:

- o If the temperature exceeds the **target_temperature_high** (25°C), the fan (or heater) will be turned on.
- o If the temperature falls below **target_temperature_low** (22°C), the heater (or fan) will be turned on.
- o If the temperature is within the desired range, the fan or heater will be turned off.

4. **Main Loop**: The program continuously checks the temperature every 10 seconds and adjusts the fan or heater accordingly.

5. **GPIO.cleanup()**: Ensures the GPIO pins are cleaned up and reset when the program is interrupted.

Step 4: Running the Code

1. Save the Python script as **smart_thermostat.py**.
2. Open a terminal and navigate to the folder where the script is saved.
3. Run the script:

```bash
bash
```

```
python3 smart_thermostat.py
```

The script will start monitoring the temperature and automatically control the fan or heater to maintain the target temperature range. It will print the current temperature and the status of the fan or heater in the terminal.

Step 5: Testing the System

1. Test the system by changing the room temperature (use a hairdryer or air conditioner to simulate temperature changes). The fan or heater should turn on when the temperature goes above or below the specified range.

2. You can modify the **target_temperature_high** and **target_temperature_low** values to customize the system according to your comfort level.

Step 6: Optional Features

To further enhance your smart thermostat system, you can add the following features:

- **Humidity control**: Use the **humidity readings** from the DHT22 sensor to control the humidity in your home by turning on a humidifier or dehumidifier.
- **Mobile or Web Interface**: Integrate a mobile app or web interface to monitor and control the temperature remotely using a **Flask** web server or a mobile app built with **Flutter** or **React Native**.

- **Schedule-based control**: Set specific times during the day when the heater or fan should be active (e.g., only during the night or when you're home).
- **Energy-saving mode**: Automatically adjust the temperature setpoint based on time of day or occupancy detected by a motion sensor.

Final Thoughts

In this chapter, you've learned how to build a **smart thermostat** with the Raspberry Pi using a **DHT22 temperature sensor** and a **relay** to control heating and cooling systems. This simple yet effective system can be customized and expanded to fit a variety of applications, such as home climate control, energy efficiency, and comfort automation.

The knowledge gained in this chapter serves as a foundation for more advanced home automation systems, where you can integrate additional sensors, create more complex control logic, and interface with other smart devices in your home.

CHAPTER 11

RASPBERRY PI FOR IOT PROJECTS

Introduction to Internet of Things (IoT) and Raspberry Pi

The **Internet of Things (IoT)** refers to the network of physical devices that are embedded with sensors, software, and other technologies, allowing them to collect, exchange, and process data. IoT enables devices to be connected to the internet and interact with each other or with users remotely. From smart homes to industrial automation, IoT has applications in almost every aspect of daily life, making things smarter, more efficient, and automated.

The **Raspberry Pi** is one of the most popular platforms for building IoT projects. Its low cost, versatility, and vast ecosystem of sensors, cameras, and accessories make it ideal for creating connected devices. With a **Raspberry Pi**, you can interface with sensors, actuators, and cloud platforms to build and deploy IoT applications.

Key Benefits of Using Raspberry Pi for IoT:

- **Low Cost**: Raspberry Pi boards are affordable and easily accessible, making them ideal for IoT prototypes.
- **Connectivity**: With built-in **Wi-Fi** and **Bluetooth**, Raspberry Pi devices can connect to the internet and communicate with other devices.
- **GPIO Pins**: Raspberry Pi's GPIO pins allow you to interface with various sensors and actuators, making it flexible for a wide range of IoT applications.
- **Open-Source Software**: Raspberry Pi uses open-source software, which allows for customization and integration with a variety of third-party tools and cloud services.

In this chapter, we will explore how to connect your Raspberry Pi to the **cloud**, enabling remote monitoring and control of your IoT devices. We will also build an example project: a **smart plant watering system** that monitors soil moisture and automatically waters a plant when it gets dry.

How to Connect Your Raspberry Pi to the Cloud

Connecting your Raspberry Pi to the cloud enables you to store, process, and analyze data remotely. It also allows you to control devices through a web interface or mobile app. Several cloud platforms can integrate seamlessly with the Raspberry Pi, including **AWS IoT**, **Google Cloud IoT**, **Microsoft Azure IoT**, and **ThingSpeak**.

We will use **ThingSpeak**, a free cloud platform for IoT applications that provides a simple way to store sensor data and access it remotely via a web interface.

Step 1: Setting Up ThingSpeak

1. **Create a ThingSpeak Account**:
   o Go to ThingSpeak and sign up for a free account.
   o After logging in, create a new **channel** for your IoT project. A channel is where your sensor data will be stored.
   o Add **fields** to your channel. For the plant watering system, create two fields:
      ▪ Field 1: Soil Moisture
      ▪ Field 2: Watering Status (On/Off)

2. **Get Your Channel API Keys**:
   o After creating your channel, go to the **API Keys** tab in the channel settings.
   o the **Write API Key**, which you will use to send data from the Raspberry Pi to ThingSpeak.

Step 2: Installing Required Libraries on Raspberry Pi

We will use Python and the **ThingSpeak** API to send data to the cloud. First, you need to install the **requests** library, which will allow your Raspberry Pi to communicate with ThingSpeak.

97

Open a terminal on your Raspberry Pi and install the `requests` library:

bash

```
sudo apt-get update
sudo apt-get install python3-requests
```

Step 3: Writing the Python Code to Send Data to ThingSpeak

In this example, we'll read the soil moisture using a **capacitive soil moisture sensor** and send the data to ThingSpeak. The system will monitor soil moisture and send the values to the cloud.

python

```
import time
import requests
import RPi.GPIO as GPIO

# Set up GPIO pins for soil moisture sensor
moisture_pin = 17  # Connect the sensor data pin
to GPIO17

# Set up ThingSpeak API endpoint and key
thingSpeakWriteKey = "YOUR_WRITE_API_KEY"
```

```
url                                        =
f"https://api.thingspeak.com/update?api_key={th
ingSpeakWriteKey}"

# Set up GPIO mode
GPIO.setmode(GPIO.BCM)
GPIO.setup(moisture_pin, GPIO.IN)

# Function to read soil moisture and send data to
ThingSpeak
def send_data_to_thingspeak(moisture_value):
    response                               =
requests.get(f"{url}&field1={moisture_value}")
    print(f"Data      sent      to      ThingSpeak:
{moisture_value}%")
    return response.status_code

# Main loop to monitor soil moisture
try:
    while True:
        # Read soil moisture level (simulated as
0 for dry and 1 for wet)
        moisture_value                     =
GPIO.input(moisture_pin)
        if moisture_value == 0:
            moisture_value = 20  # Dry soil
        else:
            moisture_value = 80  # Wet soil
```

99

```
# Send the moisture value to ThingSpeak
send_data_to_thingspeak(moisture_value)

# Wait for 60 seconds before taking
another reading
time.sleep(60)

except KeyboardInterrupt:
    print("Program interrupted")
    GPIO.cleanup()
```

Explanation of the Code:

1. **GPIO setup**: The **moisture sensor** is connected to **GPIO17**, which is read in the loop.
2. **ThingSpeak API**: The url includes your **Write API Key** and a field to send the data. We are sending the soil moisture value to **Field 1** on ThingSpeak.
3. **send_data_to_thingspeak()**: This function sends a **GET request** to ThingSpeak with the soil moisture value.
4. **Main loop**: Every 60 seconds, the system checks the soil moisture level, simulates reading the value (0 for dry and 1 for wet), and sends the data to ThingSpeak.
5. **Error Handling**: The program is set up to handle **KeyboardInterrupt** (Ctrl + C), which stops the program gracefully and cleans up the GPIO settings.

1. Save the Python script as **smart_plant_watering.py**.
2. Open a terminal and navigate to the folder where the script is saved.
3. Run the script:

```bash

python3 smart_plant_watering.py
```

The script will now start sending soil moisture data to ThingSpeak every 60 seconds. You can log into your ThingSpeak account to see the data being updated in real-time.

Example: Building a Smart Plant Watering System

Now that we've set up the cloud connectivity, let's add a relay to control a water pump that will automatically water the plant when the soil is dry. We will use a **relay module** to switch on the water pump when the soil moisture drops below a certain threshold.

Step 1: Wiring the Relay and Water Pump

1. **Relay**:

- o **VCC** to **5V** on the Raspberry Pi.
- o **GND** to **Ground**.
- o **IN** to **GPIO18** (or another GPIO pin).

2. **Water Pump**:

- o Connect the water pump to the relay. When the relay is activated, it will allow power to flow to the water pump, turning it on.

Step 2: Extending the Python Code to Control the Water Pump

Now, let's update the Python code to activate the relay (and thus the water pump) when the soil is dry.

```python
python

import time
import requests
import RPi.GPIO as GPIO

# Set up GPIO pins for soil moisture sensor and
relay
moisture_pin = 17   # Soil moisture sensor
relay_pin = 18       # Relay to control the water
pump

# Set up ThingSpeak API endpoint and key
thingSpeakWriteKey = "YOUR_WRITE_API_KEY"
```

```
url                                          =
f"https://api.thingspeak.com/update?api_key={th
ingSpeakWriteKey}"


# Set up GPIO mode
GPIO.setmode(GPIO.BCM)
GPIO.setup(moisture_pin, GPIO.IN)
GPIO.setup(relay_pin, GPIO.OUT)


# Function to send data to ThingSpeak
def send_data_to_thingspeak(moisture_value):
    response                                  =
requests.get(f"{url}&field1={moisture_value}")
    print(f"Data    sent    to    ThingSpeak:
{moisture_value}%")
    return response.status_code


# Function to control watering system
def water_plant():
    GPIO.output(relay_pin, GPIO.HIGH)  # Turn on
water pump
    print("Watering the plant...")
    time.sleep(5)  # Water for 5 seconds
    GPIO.output(relay_pin, GPIO.LOW)  # Turn off
water pump
    print("Plant watered.")


# Main loop to monitor and control watering
try:
```

```
    while True:
        # Read soil moisture level (simulated as
0 for dry and 1 for wet)
        moisture_value                    =
GPIO.input(moisture_pin)
        if moisture_value == 0:
            moisture_value = 20  # Dry soil
            water_plant()  # Water the plant if
dry
        else:
            moisture_value = 80  # Wet soil

        # Send moisture data to ThingSpeak
        send_data_to_thingspeak(moisture_value)

        # Wait for 60 seconds before checking
again
        time.sleep(60)

except KeyboardInterrupt:
    print("Program interrupted")
    GPIO.cleanup()
```

Final Thoughts

This **smart plant watering system** is a simple but effective example of how to build IoT projects with the Raspberry Pi. By connecting sensors to the cloud, you can monitor and control devices remotely. The system automatically waters the plant when the soil is dry and sends the data to the cloud for further analysis.

With this knowledge, you can expand your IoT projects to control more devices, automate your home, or even build complex industrial systems. The Raspberry Pi, with its built-in connectivity, makes it easy to connect to the cloud and create IoT solutions that improve everyday life.

CHAPTER 12

NETWORKING AND CONNECTIVITY

Setting Up a Network and Connecting Raspberry Pi to the Internet

The **Raspberry Pi** is a versatile single-board computer that supports various networking options, allowing you to connect it to the internet or local networks for IoT projects, web servers, and remote control. In this chapter, we will explore how to set up network connections on your Raspberry Pi using **Wi-Fi**, **Ethernet**, and **Bluetooth**. We'll also go over how to configure these connections to get your Raspberry Pi online and ready for various applications.

Wi-Fi Connectivity: Connecting to a Wireless Network

Most Raspberry Pi models (especially the Raspberry Pi 3 and Raspberry Pi 4) come with built-in **Wi-Fi** capabilities, making it easy to connect your Raspberry Pi to a wireless network.

Step 1: Connecting to Wi-Fi Using the Desktop Interface

1. **Power up your Raspberry Pi** and open the **Raspberry Pi OS** (formerly Raspbian).
2. In the **top-right corner** of the desktop, you'll see a **Wi-Fi icon** (two curved lines). Click on it.
3. A list of available Wi-Fi networks will appear. Select your Wi-Fi network from the list.
4. Enter your **Wi-Fi password** and click **OK**.
5. Once connected, the Wi-Fi icon will change to indicate that you're online.

Step 2: Connecting to Wi-Fi via Command Line (Headless Setup)

If you're working without a monitor (headless setup) or prefer using the command line, you can configure Wi-Fi by editing the **wpa_supplicant.conf** file.

1. Insert your Raspberry Pi's SD card into your computer.
2. Open the SD card and navigate to the **boot** directory.
3. Create a file named **wpa_supplicant.conf** with the following contents:

```bash

country=US
ctrl_interface=DIR=/var/run/wpa_supplican
t GROUP=netdev
```

```
update_config=1
network={
    ssid="YOUR_SSID"
    psk="YOUR_PASSWORD"
    key_mgmt=WPA2-PSK
}
```

4. Replace **YOUR_SSID** and **YOUR_PASSWORD** with your network's name and password.

5. Save the file and safely eject the SD card.

6. Insert the SD card back into the Raspberry Pi, power it up, and it will automatically connect to your Wi-Fi network.

Ethernet Connectivity: Connecting via a Wired Network

Connecting the Raspberry Pi to the internet using **Ethernet** is the simplest and most reliable method. If your Raspberry Pi is near a router or switch, using an Ethernet cable provides a stable, high-speed connection.

Step 1: Connect the Ethernet Cable

1. Simply plug an **Ethernet cable** into the **Ethernet port** on your Raspberry Pi and the other end into a **router or switch**.

2. The Raspberry Pi should automatically detect the wired connection and connect to the internet.

108

Step 2: Verify the Ethernet Connection

Once connected, you can verify your Ethernet connection using the terminal.

1. Open the **Terminal** on your Raspberry Pi.
2. Type the following command:

```
bash
```

```
ifconfig
```

3. Look for an interface named **eth0**. If you see an **IP address** under this interface (e.g., inet 192.168.1.x), the Raspberry Pi is successfully connected via Ethernet.

Bluetooth Connectivity: Connecting with Bluetooth Devices

The Raspberry Pi 3 and 4 also support **Bluetooth** connectivity, which allows you to connect to wireless devices such as keyboards, mice, speakers, or even other Raspberry Pi units.

Step 1: Enable Bluetooth on Raspberry Pi

1. If you're using **Raspberry Pi OS**, Bluetooth should be enabled by default.

2. To check if Bluetooth is enabled, open the terminal and run:

```bash
```

```
sudo systemctl enable bluetooth
sudo systemctl start bluetooth
```

Step 2: Pairing with Bluetooth Devices

To pair a Bluetooth device (e.g., a Bluetooth speaker, keyboard, or mouse), use the **Bluetooth Manager** in Raspberry Pi OS.

1. Open the **Bluetooth Manager** from the Raspberry Pi desktop by clicking on the **Bluetooth icon** in the taskbar.
2. Click **Add Device** and make your Raspberry Pi discoverable.
3. Select the Bluetooth device you want to pair with from the list and follow the on-screen prompts to complete the pairing process.

Step 3: Using Bluetooth via the Command Line

For headless setups or advanced users, you can manage Bluetooth connections via the terminal using the **bluez** tools.

1. To list available Bluetooth devices:

```
bash
```

```
bluetoothctl scan on
```

2. To pair with a device:

```
bash
```

```
bluetoothctl pair <device_mac_address>
```

3. To connect to the device:

```
bash
```

```
bluetoothctl connect <device_mac_address>
```

Verifying Internet Connectivity on Raspberry Pi

After setting up any of the network connections (Wi-Fi, Ethernet, Bluetooth), you can verify the internet connectivity by running:

```
bash
```

```
ping google.com
```

If the terminal responds with packets received, the Raspberry Pi is successfully connected to the internet.

Using the Raspberry Pi as a Hotspot or Bridge

In addition to basic internet connectivity, the Raspberry Pi can be used as a **Wi-Fi hotspot** or **network bridge**, which can be handy in certain IoT projects.

Step 1: Setting Up a Hotspot

1. Install the required packages:

    bash

    ```
    sudo apt-get install hostapd dnsmasq
    ```

2. Configure the **hostapd.conf** file for the Wi-Fi hotspot settings.
3. Edit the **dnsmasq.conf** file for DHCP settings.
4. Start the hotspot service using the terminal.

This setup allows your Raspberry Pi to create its own Wi-Fi network, providing internet access to other devices through its Ethernet connection or an additional Wi-Fi dongle.

Step 2: Setting Up a Bridge

If you want to bridge two networks (for example, Ethernet to Wi-Fi), you can configure the **bridge-utils** package:

1. Install the package:

```bash

sudo apt-get install bridge-utils
```

2. Configure the bridge settings using the **brctl** command and network interfaces.

Using Raspberry Pi for Remote Control and IoT Communication

The Raspberry Pi can be used for more advanced **IoT communication** with other devices via **MQTT** (Message Queuing Telemetry Transport), **HTTP**, or **WebSocket** protocols. It can communicate with cloud platforms (such as **ThingSpeak** or **AWS IoT**) to send and receive data, as well as interact with other devices on the local network.

For example:

- **MQTT** is widely used in IoT applications to send sensor data between devices.
- **HTTP** and **REST APIs** are used to fetch or send data to cloud servers.
- **WebSockets** provide real-time communication for devices that need instant updates.

113

Example: Controlling a Fan Using Web Interface

For this example, let's build a simple IoT project where you can control a fan (or any device) remotely through a web interface hosted on the Raspberry Pi. This is a basic demonstration of how to connect the Raspberry Pi to the internet and communicate with it.

1. **Set Up a Simple Flask Web Server**: Install Flask:

```bash
sudo apt-get install python3-flask
```

2. **Create the Flask App**:

```python
from flask import Flask
import RPi.GPIO as GPIO

app = Flask(__name__)

# Set up GPIO pin
fan_pin = 17
GPIO.setmode(GPIO.BCM)
GPIO.setup(fan_pin, GPIO.OUT)

@app.route("/fan_on")
```

```
def fan_on():
    GPIO.output(fan_pin, GPIO.HIGH)
    return "Fan is ON!"

@app.route("/fan_off")
def fan_off():
    GPIO.output(fan_pin, GPIO.LOW)
    return "Fan is OFF!"

if __name__ == "__main__":
    app.run(host="0.0.0.0", port=5000)
```

3. **Run the Flask App**: Save the script as **fan_control.py**, then run:

```bash

python3 fan_control.py
```

4. **Control the Fan**: Open a web browser and navigate to **http://<RaspberryPi_IP>:5000/fan_on** to turn on the fan or **http://<RaspberryPi_IP>:5000/fan_off** to turn it off.

Final Thoughts

In this chapter, we covered the basics of networking and connecting your **Raspberry Pi** to the internet using **Wi-Fi, Ethernet**, and **Bluetooth**. You learned how to send data to the cloud and create remote-controlled IoT devices using **Flask** and web interfaces.

With networking and connectivity skills in hand, you can create powerful IoT systems that can be accessed and controlled remotely from anywhere, turning your Raspberry Pi into a central hub for your smart home or IoT project.

CHAPTER 13

RASPBERRY PI CAMERA PROJECTS

Exploring the Raspberry Pi Camera Module

The **Raspberry Pi Camera Module** is a versatile and affordable camera that can be connected directly to the **Camera Serial Interface (CSI)** port on the Raspberry Pi. This camera module is ideal for a wide range of projects, from simple photography to more advanced applications like time-lapse photography, video streaming, and security monitoring.

The Raspberry Pi camera supports both still images and video recording, making it perfect for use in DIY camera systems and IoT projects. The module comes in various models, including the **standard 5 MP camera** and the newer **8 MP camera** with better resolution and quality.

Key Features of the Raspberry Pi Camera Module:

- **Resolution**: The standard camera offers 5 MP, while newer models like the **HQ Camera** offer 12 MP resolution.

- **Interface**: The camera uses the **CSI** interface, which provides high bandwidth and quality for both video and image data.
- **Compact Design**: The camera is small, lightweight, and easy to integrate into projects.
- **Wide Range of Applications**: The camera is used for projects like time-lapse photography, security systems, home automation, and machine learning applications.

Setting Up the Raspberry Pi Camera Module

Step 1: Connecting the Camera Module

1. **Power off your Raspberry Pi**.
2. Connect the **camera module** to the **CSI port** on the Raspberry Pi. Ensure that the ribbon cable is securely connected both to the **Raspberry Pi board** and the **camera module**.
3. **Power on the Raspberry Pi**.

Step 2: Enabling the Camera

1. Open a terminal on your Raspberry Pi.
2. Type the following command to open the **Raspberry Pi Configuration** menu:

```bash

sudo raspi-config
```

118

3. Navigate to **Interface Options** > **Camera** and select **Enable**.

4. After enabling the camera, reboot your Raspberry Pi:

```bash

sudo reboot
```

Step 3: Testing the Camera

After rebooting, you can test the camera by taking a photo. Run the following command:

```bash

raspistill -o test_image.jpg
```

This command will take a snapshot and save it as **test_image.jpg** in your current directory. If the camera is set up correctly, the picture will be saved, and you'll see a preview before it captures the image.

Real-World Example: Building a Time-Lapse Camera

A **time-lapse camera** is an excellent project to capture long-term changes in a scene, such as a plant growing, construction progress, or the movement of the sky. Time-lapse photography involves taking a series of photos at set intervals and then combining them into a video, which creates the appearance of accelerated motion.

In this section, we will create a **time-lapse camera system** using the Raspberry Pi camera module. The system will automatically take photos at regular intervals and store them. Afterward, you can combine the images into a time-lapse video using **FFmpeg** or any video editing software.

Components Needed:

- Raspberry Pi (any model with camera support)
- Raspberry Pi Camera Module
- MicroSD card (at least 8 GB)
- Power supply for the Raspberry Pi
- A tripod or stable surface to mount the camera (optional)

Step 1: Setting Up the Time-Lapse Code

We'll use a simple Python script to automate the process of taking photos at specific intervals.

1. Open a terminal and create a new Python script:

```bash

nano time_lapse.py
```

2. Enter the following code into the script:

```python
import time
import picamera
import os

# Set the directory to store the images
output_dir = "/home/pi/timelapse_images/"
if not os.path.exists(output_dir):
    os.makedirs(output_dir)

# Set the camera settings
camera = picamera.PICamera()

# Set the time-lapse interval and duration (in seconds)
interval = 60   # Time between each photo in seconds (1 minute)
duration = 3600  # Total duration in seconds (1 hour)

# Take pictures at the specified interval
start_time = time.time()
while time.time() - start_time < duration:
    timestamp = time.strftime("%Y%m%d-%H%M%S")
    filename = os.path.join(output_dir, f"image_{timestamp}.jpg")
```

```
camera.capture(filename)
print(f"Captured {filename}")
time.sleep(interval)


camera.close()
print("Time-lapse capture complete.")
```

Explanation of the Code:

1. **picamera.PICamera()**: This initializes the camera module to capture images.

2. **Interval**: We set the time interval between each image capture (in seconds). In this example, the camera will take a picture every minute.

3. **Duration**: The total duration for capturing images. In this example, it's set to one hour (3600 seconds).

4. **Filename**: Each image is saved with a timestamp in the format **image_YYYYMMDD-HHMMSS.jpg**, ensuring that each image is uniquely named.

5. **Capture and Sleep**: The script captures an image, saves it, and then waits for the specified interval before capturing the next photo.

6. **camera.close()**: After the time-lapse capture is complete, the camera is closed.

Step 2: Running the Time-Lapse Script

1. Save the Python script and close the editor (Ctrl + X, then Y, then Enter).

2. Run the script by typing:

```
bash
```

```
python3 time_lapse.py
```

The script will start capturing images at the specified interval and save them to the **/home/pi/timelapse_images/** directory. After the specified duration, the script will stop.

Step 3: Creating the Time-Lapse Video

Once you have a collection of images, you can use **FFmpeg** to combine the images into a time-lapse video.

1. Install **FFmpeg** if it's not already installed:

```
bash
```

```
sudo apt-get install ffmpeg
```

2. Once FFmpeg is installed, run the following command to create the video from the images:

```
bash
```

```
ffmpeg          -framerate          30          -i
/home/pi/timelapse_images/image_%Y%m%d-
```

123

```
%H%M%S.jpg -c:v libx264 -r 30 -pix_fmt yuv420p
timelapse_video.mp4
```

Explanation:

- **-framerate 30**: Specifies the frame rate of the video (30 frames per second).
- **-i image_%Y%m%d-%H%M%S.jpg**: Specifies the input file format. FFmpeg will use the timestamped images as input.
- **-c:v libx264**: Specifies the video codec to use (H.264).
- **-r 30**: Sets the frame rate of the output video.
- **-pix_fmt yuv420p**: Ensures the video is compatible with most video players.

This command will create a **timelapse_video.mp4** file that you can watch to see the time-lapse effect of the images.

Step 4: Viewing the Time-Lapse Video

Once the video has been created, you can play it on your Raspberry Pi using a video player like **VLC** or **omxplayer**:

```
bash


omxplayer timelapse_video.mp4
```

Final Thoughts

In this chapter, you've learned how to use the **Raspberry Pi Camera Module** to build a **time-lapse camera**. By taking photos at regular intervals, you can capture long-term changes in a scene and then compile them into a video for creative projects.

This foundational knowledge opens up many possibilities for Raspberry Pi camera projects, including surveillance systems, nature photography, and automated monitoring systems. You can also expand this project by integrating **motion detection** to only take pictures when something is moving, or by controlling the camera remotely via a web interface.

CHAPTER 14

SMART LIGHTING SYSTEM

Creating a System that Automates Home Lighting Based on Presence or Time of Day

A **Smart Lighting System** allows you to automate the lighting in your home based on various triggers, such as **motion detection**, **time of day**, or **presence detection**. With the **Raspberry Pi**, you can create an intelligent system that turns lights on or off when you enter a room, dims them according to ambient light, or adjusts them based on a preset schedule.

In this chapter, we will build a **Smart Lighting System** using the Raspberry Pi that:

1. Automatically turns lights on or off when motion is detected (presence-based automation).
2. Adjusts the lighting schedule based on the time of day (time-based automation).
3. Integrates with cloud services for remote control and monitoring.

This project will involve setting up a motion sensor, controlling a relay to manage the lights, and using a cloud platform for remote access.

Components Needed:

- Raspberry Pi (any model with GPIO support)
- PIR Motion Sensor (for presence detection)
- Relay Module (to control light or fan)
- LED Light or a low-power light bulb for testing (or a higher power device for real lighting control)
- Jumper wires
- Breadboard (optional, for easy connections)
- Python (for automation code)
- **Cloud service**: We will use **ThingSpeak** (or another IoT platform like **Blynk** or **AWS IoT**) to control and monitor the lights remotely.

Step 1: Wiring the Components

Wiring the PIR Motion Sensor:

1. **VCC** to **5V** (or **3.3V** depending on your sensor) on the Raspberry Pi.
2. **GND** to **Ground**.

3. **OUT** to a **GPIO pin** (e.g., **GPIO17**). This pin will detect motion.

Wiring the Relay Module:

1. **VCC** to **5V** on the Raspberry Pi.
2. **GND** to **Ground**.
3. **IN** to a **GPIO pin** (e.g., **GPIO18**). This pin will control the relay, turning the light on or off.

Step 2: Installing the Required Libraries

For this system, we'll need to install some Python libraries:

1. **RPi.GPIO** for controlling the GPIO pins.
2. **requests** for interacting with cloud services (e.g., ThingSpeak).

Install these libraries by running the following in the terminal:

```bash

sudo apt-get install python3-rpi.gpio
sudo pip3 install requests
```

Step 3: Writing the Code for the Smart Lighting System

We'll now write Python code that automates the lights based on two factors:

1. **Motion Detection**: The system will turn the light on when it detects movement and off after a certain period.
2. **Time-Based Control**: The system will turn the lights on or off at certain times of the day (e.g., during evening hours).

Create a Python file, for example, **smart_lighting.py**, and add the following code:

```python
python

import time
import RPi.GPIO as GPIO
import requests
from datetime import datetime

# Set up GPIO pins
motion_sensor_pin = 17  # GPIO pin for PIR motion
sensor
relay_pin = 18          # GPIO pin for relay
controlling the light
```

```python
# ThingSpeak configuration (for remote control)
thingSpeakWriteKey = "YOUR_WRITE_API_KEY"
url                                         =
f"https://api.thingspeak.com/update?api_key={th
ingSpeakWriteKey}"

# Set up GPIO
GPIO.setmode(GPIO.BCM)
GPIO.setup(motion_sensor_pin, GPIO.IN)    # PIR
sensor as input
GPIO.setup(relay_pin, GPIO.OUT)            # Relay
as output

# Function to control the light based on motion
def control_light_based_on_motion():
    if GPIO.input(motion_sensor_pin):    # If
motion is detected
        GPIO.output(relay_pin, GPIO.HIGH)    #
Turn on the light
        print("Motion detected! Light is ON.")
    else:
        GPIO.output(relay_pin, GPIO.LOW)  # Turn
off the light
        print("No motion detected. Light is
OFF.")

# Function to control light based on time of day
def control_light_based_on_time():
    current_time = datetime.now().hour
```

```
    if 18 <= current_time < 6:  # Example: Turn
on the light from 6 PM to 6 AM
        GPIO.output(relay_pin,   GPIO.HIGH)      #
Turn on the light
        print("It's evening! Light is ON.")
    else:
        GPIO.output(relay_pin, GPIO.LOW)  # Turn
off the light
        print("It's daytime! Light is OFF.")


# Function  to  send  status  to  ThingSpeak  for
remote monitoring
def send_status_to_thingspeak(status):
    response                                    =
requests.get(f"{url}&field1={status}")
    print(f"Sent    status    to    ThingSpeak:
{status}")
    return response.status_code


# Main loop to check for motion and time-based
control
try:
    while True:
        control_light_based_on_motion()  # Check
for motion
        control_light_based_on_time()    # Check
time and control light accordingly
```

```
        send_status_to_thingspeak("ON"          if
GPIO.input(relay_pin) == GPIO.HIGH else "OFF")   #
Send status to ThingSpeak
        time.sleep(60)   # Wait 60 seconds before
checking again

except KeyboardInterrupt:
    print("Program interrupted")
    GPIO.cleanup()   # Clean up GPIO settings on
exit
```

Explanation of the Code:

1. **GPIO Setup**: We define two GPIO pins: one for the PIR motion sensor and one for the relay.

2. **Motion Control**: The **control_light_based_on_motion()** function checks if motion is detected. If motion is detected, the light is turned on, and if there's no motion, the light is turned off.

3. **Time-Based Control**: The **control_light_based_on_time()** function checks the time of day. If it's between 6 PM and 6 AM, the light is turned on. Otherwise, it's turned off.

4. **ThingSpeak Integration**: The **send_status_to_thingspeak()** function sends the status of the light (on/off) to ThingSpeak, allowing you to monitor and control the light remotely through the ThingSpeak platform.

Step 4: Running the System

1. Save the Python script as **smart_lighting.py**.
2. Open a terminal and navigate to the directory where the script is saved.
3. Run the script:

```bash

python3 smart_lighting.py
```

The system will start running, automatically controlling the light based on motion and time of day. It will also send updates to ThingSpeak every 60 seconds.

Step 5: Integrating with Cloud Services for Remote Control

We've already integrated the system with **ThingSpeak**, a cloud platform that allows you to monitor and control the light remotely.

1. **ThingSpeak**: Using the **ThingSpeak API**, you can control the light remotely. For example, you can create a web interface or a mobile app that allows you to turn the light on or off, regardless of your location.

   To test remote control:

   o Go to your ThingSpeak channel's **API Keys** section and make sure you have the **Write API Key**.

   o You can use the following URL to update the light status manually:

   ```bash
   https://api.thingspeak.com/update?api_key=YOUR_WRITE_API_KEY&field1=ON
   ```

   o Replace **YOUR_WRITE_API_KEY** with your actual ThingSpeak API key and change the `field1` value to "OFF" to turn off the light remotely.

2. **Other Cloud Services**: You can use other platforms like **Blynk**, **Google Cloud IoT**, or **AWS IoT** to monitor and control the system. Most of these platforms offer mobile apps for remote control,

which can be easily integrated with your Raspberry Pi projects.

Final Thoughts

In this chapter, we've created a **Smart Lighting System** using the Raspberry Pi, integrating **motion detection** and **time-based automation** for intelligent lighting control. Additionally, we've connected the system to the **ThingSpeak cloud platform**, enabling **remote monitoring and control** of the lights.

This project is just the beginning of what you can do with Raspberry Pi and home automation. By adding more sensors, schedules, or integrating with smart home ecosystems like **Google Home** or **Amazon Alexa**, you can build a fully connected home. From controlling lights to managing security systems, the possibilities for automation with the Raspberry Pi are endless.

CHAPTER 15

BUILDING A SMART MIRROR

Creating an Interactive Smart Mirror Using a Raspberry Pi and a Two-Way Mirror

A **Smart Mirror** is an interactive display that serves as both a mirror and a smart device. It typically displays useful information, such as the time, date, weather, news, calendar, or even traffic updates. With the **Raspberry Pi**, a **two-way mirror**, and a few other components, you can create your own Smart Mirror that seamlessly integrates into your home.

In this chapter, we will build a **Smart Mirror** using the Raspberry Pi that:

1. Displays **time** and **date**.
2. Shows **weather information**.
3. Displays a **calendar** or any other custom information you choose.

The mirror will work like a regular mirror when it's not displaying information, but when turned on, the Raspberry Pi will show the data overlaid on the mirror surface.

Step 1: Materials Needed

To build a Smart Mirror, you will need the following components:

- **Raspberry Pi** (any model, but Raspberry Pi 3 or later recommended)
- **Two-way mirror** (a reflective mirror with transparency, which will allow the screen to display through it)
- **HDMI monitor** (with a screen size that fits the frame of your mirror)
- **Frame** for the mirror (you can use a picture frame or custom frame)
- **MicroSD card** (at least 8GB, with Raspberry Pi OS installed)
- **Power supply** for the Raspberry Pi
- **Keyboard and Mouse** (for initial setup)
- **Wi-Fi or Ethernet connection** (for internet access)
- **Python** (for code to display the content)
- **MagicMirror software** (open-source platform for smart mirrors)
- **USB webcam** (optional, for additional interactive features like facial recognition or voice control)

Step 2: Assembling the Physical Smart Mirror

1. **Prepare the Frame**:

   o Find or create a frame that will house the monitor and the two-way mirror. The frame should fit your display screen and allow the two-way mirror to sit in front of it.

2. **Install the Two-Way Mirror**:

   o Place the **two-way mirror** in front of the screen, ensuring it's centered. The mirror should be clear enough for the Raspberry Pi's display to show through, but reflective enough to work as a normal mirror when not displaying content.

3. **Position the Raspberry Pi and Monitor**:

   o Mount the **Raspberry Pi** and the monitor securely within the frame. The monitor will act as the display, and the two-way mirror will sit in front of it, creating the "smart" effect.

   o Ensure the Raspberry Pi is connected to the **monitor via HDMI** and the power supply is connected.

Step 3: Setting Up the Raspberry Pi and Installing MagicMirror Software

1. **Set Up Raspberry Pi OS**:

- o If you haven't already, download and install **Raspberry Pi OS** onto your **microSD card** using **Raspberry Pi Imager**. Insert the microSD card into the Raspberry Pi.
- o Boot up the Raspberry Pi and go through the initial setup process (language, Wi-Fi, updates).

2. **Install Dependencies**: The **MagicMirror** software is open-source and free to use. To install MagicMirror, you will need to use the terminal.

- o First, open the terminal and install some required software dependencies:

```
bash

sudo apt-get update
sudo apt-get upgrade
sudo  apt-get  install  -y  python3-dev
python3-pip git
```

3. **Clone the MagicMirror Repository**: MagicMirror provides a customizable platform for building smart mirrors. Clone the repository from GitHub:

```
bash

cd ~
git                                    clone
https://github.com/MichMich/MagicMirror
```

```
cd MagicMirror
```

4. **Install MagicMirror**: Once the repository is cloned, run the installation script to set up the software:

```
bash
```

```
bash install.sh
```

This will install all the necessary components, including **Node.js** and **Electron**, which are required to run the MagicMirror software.

Step 4: Configuring MagicMirror to Display Information

1. **Configure MagicMirror**: MagicMirror uses a configuration file where you can specify which modules (time, weather, calendar, news, etc.) you want to display.

   o Navigate to the **config** folder:

   ```
   bash
   ```

   ```
   cd ~/MagicMirror/config
   ```

140

o Open the **config.js** file to modify the settings:

```bash
```

```
nano config.js
```

2. **Add Default Modules**: MagicMirror comes with a number of pre-configured modules. You can add modules for displaying:

   o **Time**: Shows the current time and date.
   o **Weather**: Displays the current weather based on your location.
   o **Calendar**: Shows upcoming events from your Google Calendar or other sources.
   o **News**: Displays headlines from your favorite news sources.

For example, to display the time, ensure the following module is enabled:

```javascript
{
  module: "clock",
  position: "top_left",
  config: {
    timeFormat: "12",
    displaySeconds: true
```

141

```
    }
},
```

For weather, you will need an **API key** from a weather service like **OpenWeatherMap**. In the config.js file, find the weather module section and add your API key:

```
javascript
```

```
{
  module: "weather",
  position: "top_right",
  config: {
    location: "London", // Change to your
location
    locationID: "",     // Location ID from
OpenWeatherMap
    appid: "YOUR_API_KEY" // Replace with
your API key
  }
},
```

If you want to display your calendar, you can configure the **calendar module** to show events from your **Google Calendar**.

Step 5: Starting the Magic Mirror

1. **Start MagicMirror**: Once the configuration is done, you can start the MagicMirror software. Run the following command to launch it:

```bash

npm start
```

This will open the MagicMirror interface in **Electron** (a framework for building desktop applications). The system should now be displaying the information overlaid on the two-way mirror.

2. **Set MagicMirror to Start on Boot**: To ensure that the MagicMirror system starts automatically when the Raspberry Pi is powered on, you can configure it to run at startup.

Run the following command:

```bash

sudo nano /etc/rc.local
```

Add the following line just before the `exit 0` line:

143

```
bash

sudo        -u        pi        DISPLAY=:0
/home/pi/MagicMirror/installers/mm.sh
```

Save the file and exit. Now, when the Raspberry Pi starts, it will automatically run the MagicMirror system.

Step 6: Customizing Your Smart Mirror

You can enhance and customize your Smart Mirror by adding additional modules, such as:

- **Voice Control**: Integrate **Google Assistant** or **Alexa** to control your Smart Mirror with voice commands.
- **Facial Recognition**: Add a facial recognition module to greet specific people or show custom content based on who is in front of the mirror.
- **News Feeds**: Integrate custom RSS feeds or display social media updates.
- **Time-lapse Camera**: Integrate the Raspberry Pi camera to display a live feed or time-lapse video behind the mirror.

You can also customize the **appearance** of the mirror's interface by modifying the **CSS** files in the **MagicMirror** directories.

Final Thoughts

In this chapter, we've created a **Smart Mirror** that displays useful information such as the **time**, **weather**, and **calendar** on a reflective surface. Using the **Raspberry Pi**, **MagicMirror**, and a **two-way mirror**, you can create an interactive and functional smart mirror for your home.

The possibilities for customizing your Smart Mirror are endless. By adding more sensors, integrating voice control, or even adding custom modules, you can make the mirror serve as a smart home hub. Whether it's used for checking the weather, managing your schedule, or controlling your smart home devices, the Raspberry Pi Smart Mirror is an excellent starting point for building innovative IoT projects.

CHAPTER 16

SECURITY SYSTEMS WITH RASPBERRY PI

Building a Home Security System with Motion Sensors, Cameras, and Alarms

A **home security system** is an essential part of any smart home, providing peace of mind by monitoring the premises for intrusions and responding to potential threats. With a **Raspberry Pi**, you can build a customizable and affordable security system using various sensors, cameras, and alarms. This chapter will focus on how to create a **door/window alarm system** that uses **motion sensors**, a **camera module**, and an **alarm** to detect unauthorized access and alert you.

We'll also discuss the basics of building a more complex security system, and how to integrate it with your home network and mobile app for remote monitoring.

Components Needed:

- Raspberry Pi (any model with GPIO support)
- PIR Motion Sensor (for detecting movement)
- Magnetic Contact Switches (for doors/windows)

- Relay Module (to control the alarm or siren)
- Buzzer or Siren (for the alarm)
- Raspberry Pi Camera Module (for taking pictures/videos upon detection)
- Jumper wires
- Breadboard (optional, for easy connections)
- MicroSD card with Raspberry Pi OS installed
- Python (for coding the security system)

Step 1: Setting Up the Hardware

1. Connecting the PIR Motion Sensor

The **PIR (Passive Infrared) Motion Sensor** detects movement by sensing infrared radiation from warm objects, like humans. When a person enters the sensor's detection range, it sends a signal to the Raspberry Pi to trigger an alarm.

- **VCC** to **5V** or **3.3V** on the Raspberry Pi (depending on your sensor model).
- **GND** to **Ground**.
- **OUT** to a **GPIO pin** (e.g., **GPIO17**) on the Raspberry Pi.

2. Connecting the Magnetic Door/Window Contact Switch

The **magnetic contact switch** is used to detect whether a door or window is open or closed. The switch is made up of two parts: one part is attached to the door/window frame, and the other part is attached to the door or window. When the door/window is closed, the two parts are in contact, but when opened, the circuit is broken.

- One lead of the contact switch goes to **5V** or **3.3V** on the Raspberry Pi.
- The other lead goes to a **GPIO pin** (e.g., **GPIO18**) on the Raspberry Pi.
- When the door/window is open, the switch will send a signal to the Raspberry Pi.

3. Connecting the Relay Module (for Alarm Control)

The **Relay Module** allows the Raspberry Pi to control high-voltage devices like an **alarm siren** or **buzzer**.

- **VCC** to **5V** on the Raspberry Pi.
- **GND** to **Ground**.
- **IN** to a **GPIO pin** (e.g., **GPIO19**) on the Raspberry Pi.

Connect the **NO (Normally Open)** terminal of the relay to the **alarm**'s power input, and the **COM (Common)** terminal to the **alarm's ground**.

4. Setting Up the Raspberry Pi Camera

To capture video or images when an intrusion is detected, use the **Raspberry Pi Camera Module**. The camera module connects to the **Camera Serial Interface (CSI)** port on the Raspberry Pi.

- Connect the camera module to the **CSI port** on the Raspberry Pi.
- Enable the camera interface on the Raspberry Pi by running `sudo raspi-config` and selecting **Interface Options > Camera > Enable**.

Step 2: Writing the Security System Code

We'll write Python code that:

1. Monitors the PIR motion sensor and door/window contact switch.
2. Activates an alarm when motion or door/window opening is detected.

3. Captures a photo or video with the camera to document the event.

Here's the code for the system:

```python

import RPi.GPIO as GPIO
import time
import picamera
from datetime import datetime

# Set up GPIO pins
motion_sensor_pin = 17   # PIR sensor GPIO pin
contact_switch_pin = 18   # Door/window contact switch GPIO pin
relay_pin = 19  # Relay for controlling the alarm

# Set up the camera
camera = picamera.PICamera()

# Set up GPIO
GPIO.setmode(GPIO.BCM)
GPIO.setup(motion_sensor_pin, GPIO.IN)   # Motion sensor input
GPIO.setup(contact_switch_pin, GPIO.IN)     # Door/window switch input
GPIO.setup(relay_pin, GPIO.OUT)    # Relay to control alarm
```

```
# Function to capture an image when an alarm is
triggered
def capture_image():
    timestamp = time.strftime("%Y%m%d-%H%M%S")
    filename                                  =
f"/home/pi/security_photos/{timestamp}.jpg"
    camera.capture(filename)
    print(f"Image captured: {filename}")


# Function to activate the alarm
def activate_alarm():
    GPIO.output(relay_pin, GPIO.HIGH)  # Turn on
the alarm
    print("Alarm activated!")
    capture_image()  # Capture an image
    time.sleep(10)  # Keep the alarm on for 10
seconds
    GPIO.output(relay_pin, GPIO.LOW)  # Turn off
the alarm
    print("Alarm deactivated!")


# Function to check the door/window status
def check_contact_switch():
    if    GPIO.input(contact_switch_pin)    ==
GPIO.LOW:  # Contact switch open (door/window
open)
        print("Door/Window    open!    Triggering
alarm.")
```

```
        activate_alarm()

# Main loop
try:
    while True:
        if GPIO.input(motion_sensor_pin):   # If
motion is detected
            print("Motion  detected!  Triggering
alarm.")
            activate_alarm()

        check_contact_switch()   # Check if the
door/window is open
        time.sleep(1)   # Check every second for
motion or door/window status

except KeyboardInterrupt:
    print("Program interrupted")
    GPIO.cleanup()   # Clean up GPIO settings on
exit
```

Explanation of the Code:

1. **GPIO Setup**: We configure the **motion sensor**, **contact switch**, and **relay** as input and output pins.

2. **capture_image()**: When the system detects an intruder, it captures an image using the Raspberry Pi camera. The image is saved with a timestamp to a directory on the Raspberry Pi.

152

3. **activate_alarm()**: This function turns on the alarm (using the relay) for 10 seconds and then turns it off. It also captures an image.

4. **check_contact_switch()**: This function checks the door/window contact switch to determine if the door/window is open. If the switch is open, it triggers the alarm.

5. The **main loop** constantly checks for motion and door/window status. If either is triggered, the alarm is activated.

Step 3: Running the Security System

1. **Create the directory** to store the images:

bash

```
mkdir /home/pi/security_photos
```

2. **Run the security system**: Save the Python script as **security_system.py** and run it:

bash

```
python3 security_system.py
```

The system will start monitoring for motion or an open door/window. If an intrusion is detected, the alarm will activate, and the camera will capture an image.

Step 4: Expanding the Security System

You can expand the system by adding more sensors or integrating additional features:

- **Multiple cameras**: Add more cameras to monitor different areas of your home.
- **Email or SMS alerts**: Integrate services like **Twilio** or **SendGrid** to send real-time alerts when an intrusion is detected.
- **Cloud storage**: Upload images or videos to cloud platforms like **Google Drive** or **AWS S3** for remote access and storage.
- **Web interface**: Set up a web server (e.g., using **Flask**) to monitor and control the security system remotely.

Final Thoughts

In this chapter, we built a simple but effective **home security system** using the **Raspberry Pi**, **motion sensors**, **camera modules**, and **alarms**. We created an automated system that detects intrusions, triggers alarms, and captures images or videos to document the event.

With the Raspberry Pi's GPIO pins and a variety of sensors, you can create a highly customizable and affordable security system for your home. By integrating additional features like cloud storage, real-time alerts, and remote monitoring, you can further enhance the functionality and accessibility of your security system.

CHAPTER 17

VOICE-ACTIVATED CONTROL SYSTEMS

Integrating Voice Assistants like Google Assistant or Alexa with Raspberry Pi

Voice-activated control systems have become increasingly popular in home automation, allowing users to control devices with just their voice. With the **Raspberry Pi**, you can integrate **voice assistants** like **Google Assistant** or **Amazon Alexa** to build voice-controlled systems for home automation. Whether you want to control your lights, thermostat, or security system, voice assistants provide a convenient way to interact with your smart home.

In this chapter, we will:

1. Explore how to set up **Google Assistant** and **Amazon Alexa** on a Raspberry Pi.
2. Use these voice assistants to build a **voice-activated home automation system** that can control smart devices like lights, fans, and thermostats.

Step 1: Setting Up Google Assistant on Raspberry Pi

Google Assistant is a powerful voice assistant that can be integrated into the Raspberry Pi using the **Google Assistant SDK**. The SDK allows you to send voice commands to the Google Assistant and receive responses directly on the Raspberry Pi.

1. Setting Up Google Assistant SDK

Here's how to set up Google Assistant on your Raspberry Pi:

1. **Prepare your Raspberry Pi**:
   o Install **Raspberry Pi OS** and ensure it is up to date.
   o Make sure you have access to **Wi-Fi** or **Ethernet** for network connectivity.

2. **Enable Google Assistant API**:
   o Go to the **Google Cloud Console**: https://console.cloud.google.com
   o Create a new **project**.
   o Navigate to **APIs & Services** > **Library**.
   o Search for **Google Assistant API** and enable it for your project.

o Go to the **Credentials** tab and create **OAuth 2.0 credentials**. Download the credentials file (credentials.json).

3. **Install Dependencies**: Open the terminal on your Raspberry Pi and install the necessary dependencies:

bash

```
sudo apt-get update
sudo apt-get install python3-dev python3-
venv python3-pip
sudo apt-get install portaudio19-dev
libffi-dev libssl-dev
sudo apt-get install libmpg123-dev
```

4. **Install Google Assistant SDK**: Set up a virtual environment to install the SDK:

bash

```
python3 -m venv assistant-env
source assistant-env/bin/activate
pip install --upgrade google-assistant-
sdk[samples]
```

5. **Authenticate Your Google Assistant**: Run the authentication command:

bash

158

```
google-oauthlib-tool      --client-secrets
credentials.json                --scope
https://www.googleapis.com/auth/assistant
-sdk-prototype --save --headless
```

Follow the instructions to authenticate and get an **authorization code**.

6. **Run Google Assistant**: After the setup, run the following command to test if Google Assistant is working:

```
bash
```

```
googlesamples-assistant-pushtotalk      --
project-id   <your_project_id>   --device-
model-id <your_device_model_id>
```

Now, you can use the Raspberry Pi's microphone to give voice commands, and Google Assistant will respond.

Step 2: Setting Up Amazon Alexa on Raspberry Pi

Amazon Alexa is another popular voice assistant that you can integrate with the Raspberry Pi. The **Alexa Voice**

Service (AVS) allows you to use Alexa on devices like the Raspberry Pi.

1. Setting Up Alexa Voice Service (AVS) on Raspberry Pi

Here's how to set up Alexa on your Raspberry Pi:

1. **Sign Up for Amazon Developer Account**:
   - Go to the **Amazon Developer Portal**: https://developer.amazon.com
   - Sign in or create an account.
   - Navigate to **Alexa** > **Alexa Voice Service** and create a new product under **AVS**.
   - Create a **security profile** and download the **Client ID** and **Client Secret**.

2. **Install Dependencies**: Open the terminal and install the necessary dependencies:

```bash
sudo apt-get update
sudo apt-get install git cmake build-essential libssl-dev
sudo apt-get install libpulse-dev libasound2-dev
sudo apt-get install libcurl4-openssl-dev
```

3. **Clone the Alexa SDK**: Clone the **Alexa SDK** repository to your Raspberry Pi:

```bash
```

```bash
git clone https://github.com/alexa/avs-
device-sdk.git
cd avs-device-sdk
```

4. **Build the SDK**: Compile and build the Alexa SDK:

```bash
```

```bash
mkdir build
cd build
cmake ..
make
sudo make install
```

5. **Configure the SDK**: Follow the instructions in the **Alexa SDK Documentation** to configure the **config.json** file and use the **Client ID** and **Client Secret** you obtained from Amazon.

6. **Run Alexa**: After configuration, run the following command to start the Alexa service:

```bash
```

161

```
./bin/Release/avs-device-sdk --config-file
/path/to/your/config.json
```

You should now have Alexa running on your Raspberry Pi. It will listen to voice commands and respond accordingly.

Step 3: Creating a Voice-Activated Home Automation System

Now that you have **Google Assistant** and **Alexa** set up on your Raspberry Pi, we will integrate them into a **voice-activated home automation system**. The system will allow you to control **smart lights**, **thermostats**, and other devices using voice commands.

1. Setting Up Smart Lights with Voice Commands

To control lights, you can use **smart light bulbs** like **Philips Hue** or **LIFX**, or you can use a **relay module** to control regular lights. Here's an example of controlling a smart light:

Using Google Assistant with Smart Lights:

- With Google Assistant enabled, say something like:

bash

162

```
"Hey Google, turn on the living room
lights."
```

- If your smart lights are connected to your Google Home, they will turn on.

Using Alexa with Smart Lights:

- With Alexa enabled, say:

```
bash
```

```
"Alexa, turn off the kitchen light."
```

- Your Alexa-enabled smart lights will respond accordingly.

2. Integrating the Relay Module for Non-Smart Lights

If you're using a regular light and want to control it using a relay (for example, via a Raspberry Pi GPIO pin), you can set up a simple Python script that controls the relay when it receives a voice command from **Google Assistant** or **Alexa**.

For example, let's integrate a **smart light relay** with Google Assistant:

1. **Wiring the Relay**:

- o Connect the **relay** to **GPIO17** on the Raspberry Pi.
- o Connect the light (or fan) to the relay.

2. **Python Code to Control Relay**: Here's a basic Python script to turn on/off the relay:

```python
import RPi.GPIO as GPIO
import time

# Set up the GPIO pin for the relay
GPIO.setmode(GPIO.BCM)
relay_pin = 17
GPIO.setup(relay_pin, GPIO.OUT)

def turn_on_light():
    GPIO.output(relay_pin, GPIO.HIGH)  # Turn on the light
    print("Light is ON")

def turn_off_light():
    GPIO.output(relay_pin, GPIO.LOW)  # Turn off the light
    print("Light is OFF")

# Main loop to handle voice commands (simplified)
while True:
```

```
command       =       input("Enter       command:
").strip().lower()
    if command == "turn on light":
        turn_on_light()
    elif command == "turn off light":
        turn_off_light()
    time.sleep(1)
```

3. **Integrating with Google Assistant**: Use the Google Assistant or Alexa to issue voice commands. For example, when you say "Hey Google, turn on the light," the system can call the `turn_on_light()` function from the script.

Step 4: Expanding Your Voice-Activated System

- **Voice-Controlled Thermostat**: Integrate a smart thermostat like **Nest** or a DIY temperature sensor with Google Assistant or Alexa to adjust the temperature using voice commands.

- **Security System Integration**: Add motion detectors or cameras, and control them using voice commands. For example, "Alexa, show the front door camera" or "Hey Google, activate security mode."

- **Scene Management**: Use voice commands to control multiple devices at once. For example, "Alexa, good night" to turn off lights, lock doors, and set the thermostat.

Final Thoughts

In this chapter, we have learned how to set up **voice assistants** like **Google Assistant** and **Amazon Alexa** on the Raspberry Pi and integrate them into a **voice-activated home automation system**. With voice control, you can easily manage smart devices like lights, thermostats, and even security systems with simple voice commands.

By combining **Raspberry Pi**, **voice assistants**, and IoT devices, you can build a fully voice-controlled smart home system. Expanding the system with additional devices, sensors, and services allows you to create a truly connected home.

CHAPTER 18

RASPBERRY PI AS A MEDIA CENTER

Setting up Raspberry Pi as a Home Theater System with Kodi or Plex

The **Raspberry Pi** is a powerful, low-cost device that can be transformed into a full-fledged **media center**. With the right software, you can use the Raspberry Pi to stream movies, TV shows, music, and even display photos on your TV or projector, making it an ideal choice for a **home theater system**.

In this chapter, we'll cover how to set up the Raspberry Pi as a media center using two popular media server software solutions: **Kodi** and **Plex**. Both Kodi and Plex allow you to stream and manage your media collection, but each has its unique features and setup processes.

We will also explore how to **stream movies** and **music** using the Raspberry Pi, turning it into a central hub for all your entertainment needs.

167

Step 1: Setting Up Kodi on Raspberry Pi

Kodi is a free and open-source media player and entertainment hub that is easy to set up on the Raspberry Pi. It provides a simple, user-friendly interface for accessing media content and supports various file formats for videos, music, and images.

1. Install Kodi on Raspberry Pi

The easiest way to get Kodi running on your Raspberry Pi is by using **LibreELEC**, a lightweight operating system that comes pre-installed with Kodi. LibreELEC is designed specifically for media center use, offering a fast and responsive system.

Installing LibreELEC:

1. Download **LibreELEC** from the official website: https://libreelec.tv/
2. Use the **Raspberry Pi Imager** to write the LibreELEC image to your **microSD card**:
   o Open the **Raspberry Pi Imager**, choose the **LibreELEC** image, and select your SD card.

o   Click **Write** to install LibreELEC to the microSD card.

3. After the installation is complete, insert the microSD card into your Raspberry Pi and power it on.

4. **Configure Kodi**:

   o   When Kodi boots up, you'll be greeted with a user interface.

   o   Follow the on-screen prompts to complete the **initial setup**, including configuring your **Wi-Fi** and **language preferences**.

5. Once Kodi is installed, you can use it to access and play movies, TV shows, and music. The system supports a wide range of media formats and is highly customizable.

2. Setting Up Media Sources in Kodi

To stream movies or music from your local storage or network, you need to add media sources to Kodi.

1. From the Kodi main menu, go to **Videos** > **Files** > **Add Videos**.

2. Select **Browse**, and navigate to the folder containing your media files.

3. Choose the **folder** and **name** the source (e.g., "Movies" or "Music").

4. Click **OK** to add the source.

You can also stream media from a network drive or NAS (Network Attached Storage) by adding the appropriate network path in the **Add Source** menu.

3. Accessing Streaming Services in Kodi

Kodi supports various add-ons that allow you to access streaming services like **YouTube**, **Netflix**, **Spotify**, and others. To install add-ons:

1. From the Kodi home screen, go to **Add-ons**.
2. Select **Install from repository**.
3. Browse the **official Kodi repository** or other third-party repositories to install popular streaming services.
4. Once installed, you can access these services directly through Kodi.

Step 2: Setting Up Plex on Raspberry Pi

Plex is a popular media server platform that allows you to organize and stream your media collection to various devices, including smartphones, tablets, and smart TVs. Plex offers a client-server model, where the **Plex Media Server**

runs on your Raspberry Pi, and you can use the **Plex app** on your phone, tablet, or TV to access and stream content.

1. Install Plex Media Server on Raspberry Pi

Setting up Plex on the Raspberry Pi is straightforward. Here's how you can do it:

1. **Install Plex Media Server**: Open a terminal on your Raspberry Pi and run the following commands:

```bash
sudo apt-get update
sudo apt-get install apt-transport-https
sudo curl https://downloads.plex.tv/plex-keys/PlexSign.key | sudo apt-key add -
sudo echo "deb https://downloads.plex.tv/repo/deb public main" > /etc/apt/sources.list.d/plex.list
sudo apt-get update
sudo apt-get install plexmediaserver
```

2. **Start Plex Media Server**: After installing Plex, you can start the Plex Media Server by running the following command:

```bash
```

171

```
sudo service plexmediaserver start
```

3. **Access Plex Web Interface**: Once Plex is installed, you can access the Plex web interface by opening a browser on your Raspberry Pi or any device on the same network and navigating to:

```
arduino
```

```
http://<raspberry_pi_ip>:32400/web
```

4. **Set Up Your Library**: The web interface will guide you through the setup process, where you can add your media libraries (Movies, TV Shows, Music, etc.).

   o Select **Libraries** and choose the type (e.g., **Movies** or **Music**).
   o Point Plex to the folder containing your media files.

5. **Install Plex App on Client Devices**: You can install the Plex app on various devices, such as smartphones, smart TVs, and streaming devices (e.g., Chromecast, Roku, Apple TV).

   o Use the **Plex app** to stream content from your Raspberry Pi to these devices.

172

Step 3: Streaming Movies and Music with Raspberry Pi

1. Streaming Movies with Kodi or Plex

- **Kodi**: Once you've added your media sources, you can easily browse and play movies by selecting **Videos** > **Movies** from the main menu.
- **Plex**: Open the Plex app on your phone, tablet, or smart TV. Browse your libraries and start streaming movies directly from your Raspberry Pi.

Both Kodi and Plex support a wide range of video formats, including **MKV**, **MP4**, **AVI**, and more. Additionally, they both support streaming over the network, so you can access your media from anywhere in your home.

2. Streaming Music with Kodi or Plex

- **Kodi**: You can add a music source by going to **Music** > **Files** > **Add Music**. Once added, you can browse and play your music collection.
- **Plex**: Similarly, Plex allows you to stream music by adding it to your **Music Library**. Plex will automatically

organize your music and allow you to browse by artist, album, genre, or even create playlists.

Both platforms support **metadata fetching**, which means they will automatically download album art, artist bios, and other information for your music library.

Step 4: Enhancing the Media Center Experience

1. Remote Control for Kodi

You can control Kodi remotely using the **Kodi Remote App** available for both **iOS** and **Android**. This allows you to control playback, browse your media, and adjust settings from your mobile device.

2. Voice Control with Google Assistant or Alexa

You can integrate voice assistants like **Google Assistant** or **Amazon Alexa** with Kodi or Plex to control your media center. For example, you could say:

- "Alexa, play a movie on Plex."
- "Hey Google, play music on Kodi."

3. Streaming to Other Devices

With **Plex**, you can stream your content to other devices in your home, such as smart TVs, computers, smartphones, and tablets. **Kodi** also has streaming capabilities through **UPnP** (Universal Plug and Play) or **DLNA** (Digital Living Network Alliance) to stream media across your network.

Final Thoughts

In this chapter, we've transformed the **Raspberry Pi** into a powerful **media center** using **Kodi** and **Plex**. Both solutions offer robust features for streaming movies, TV shows, music, and more, turning your Raspberry Pi into the heart of your home entertainment system.

Whether you prefer the customizable interface of **Kodi** or the client-server setup of **Plex**, both provide excellent options for enjoying your media collection. You can further enhance the experience by adding **voice control**, **remote access**, and streaming to **multiple devices**, making the Raspberry Pi a versatile media hub.

CHAPTER 19

CREATING A PERSONAL WEB SERVER

Turning Your Raspberry Pi into a Local Web Server Using Apache or Nginx

A **web server** is a software that serves content, such as websites, blogs, or applications, to users over the internet. The **Raspberry Pi** is an excellent platform for hosting a personal web server due to its low cost, energy efficiency, and flexibility.

In this chapter, we will explore how to turn your Raspberry Pi into a **local web server** using two of the most popular web server software options: **Apache** and **Nginx**. We'll also create a simple example of hosting a **blog** or **website** using **Apache** or **Nginx**.

Step 1: Choosing a Web Server: Apache vs. Nginx

176

Apache and **Nginx** are two of the most widely used web server platforms. Both have their advantages, and the choice between them depends on the specific needs of your project:

- **Apache** is a more traditional and feature-rich web server. It is easy to set up and is widely used for hosting dynamic content (e.g., WordPress or other content management systems).
- **Nginx** is a modern and lightweight web server designed for high performance and scalability. It's often used for serving static content (e.g., HTML, CSS, images) and is popular for its ability to handle high traffic with low resource usage.

For this chapter, we'll use **Apache** as it's easier for beginners to set up and works well with a variety of web applications.

Step 2: Setting Up Apache Web Server on Raspberry Pi

Apache is one of the most widely used web servers and can be easily set up on the Raspberry Pi.

1. Install Apache on Raspberry Pi

To install Apache, follow these steps:

1. Open a terminal on your Raspberry Pi and update the package list:

```bash
sudo apt-get update
```

2. Install Apache using the following command:

```bash
sudo apt-get install apache2 -y
```

3. After the installation is complete, Apache will start automatically. You can verify it by opening your Raspberry Pi's IP address in a web browser:

```bash
http://<RaspberryPi_IP>
```

You should see the default Apache welcome page that confirms Apache is working.

2. Configure Apache

Apache's configuration files are located in the `/etc/apache2/` directory. The main configuration file is **apache2.conf**, and the default website files are stored in `/var/www/html`.

To test your Apache server, you can modify the default HTML file:

1. Navigate to the Apache root directory:

```bash

cd /var/www/html
```

2. Edit the **index.html** file:

```bash

sudo nano index.html
```

3. Change the content to something simple, like:

```html

<html>
    <head>
```

```
        <title>My    Raspberry    Pi    Web
Server</title>
    </head>
    <body>
        <h1>Welcome   to   my   personal   web
server!</h1>
    </body>
</html>
```

4. Save and exit the editor (Ctrl + X, then Y, and Enter).

Now, when you go to your Raspberry Pi's IP address in a web browser, you should see your custom webpage.

3. Set Up a Simple Blog or Website

To create a simple **blog** or **website**, you can install **WordPress** or simply create a basic static website.

Example: Installing WordPress

1. Install the necessary dependencies (PHP, MySQL, etc.):

bash

```
sudo apt-get install php libapache2-mod-
php mysql-server php-mysql -y
```

2. Download and extract the latest version of **WordPress**:

bash

```
cd /var/www/html
sudo                            wget
https://wordpress.org/latest.tar.gz
sudo tar -xvzf latest.tar.gz
sudo mv wordpress/* .
sudo rmdir wordpress
```

3. Set up the **MySQL database** for WordPress:

bash

```
sudo mysql -u root -p
```

Inside the MySQL shell, create a new database and user for WordPress:

sql

```
CREATE DATABASE wordpress;
CREATE     USER     'wpuser'@'localhost'
IDENTIFIED BY 'password';
GRANT ALL PRIVILEGES ON wordpress.* TO
'wpuser'@'localhost';
FLUSH PRIVILEGES;
```

```
EXIT;
```

4. Open the **WordPress configuration file** and set up the database details:

```bash
sudo cp wp-config-sample.php wp-config.php
sudo nano wp-config.php
```

Update the database name, username, and password as follows:

```php
define( 'DB_NAME', 'wordpress' );
define( 'DB_USER', 'wpuser' );
define( 'DB_PASSWORD', 'password' );
```

5. Finally, open your Raspberry Pi's IP address in a web browser:

```bash
http://<RaspberryPi_IP>
```

You will be guided through the WordPress setup process where you can choose a site name, admin username, and password.

182

Step 3: Setting Up Nginx Web Server (Alternative Option)

While Apache is easier for beginners, **Nginx** offers superior performance for handling static content. If you want a lighter web server, you can set up **Nginx** on your Raspberry Pi.

1. Install Nginx

To install Nginx, run the following commands:

1. Update package lists:

    ```bash
    sudo apt-get update
    ```

2. Install Nginx:

    ```bash
    sudo apt-get install nginx -y
    ```

3. Once installed, you can check Nginx by visiting your Raspberry Pi's IP address in a browser:

```bash
```

```
http://<RaspberryPi_IP>
```

You should see the default Nginx welcome page.

2. Configure Nginx

To configure Nginx, modify the **default configuration** file:

1. Open the configuration file:

```bash
```

```
sudo          nano          /etc/nginx/sites-
available/default
```

2. Edit the **server block** to define the root directory for your website:

```nginx
```

```
server {
    listen 80;
    server_name _;

    root /var/www/html;
    index       index.html       index.htm
index.nginx-debian.html;
```

184

```
location / {
    try_files $uri $uri/ =404;
}
}
```

3. Test the configuration:

```
bash
```

```
sudo nginx -t
```

4. Restart Nginx to apply the changes:

```
bash
```

```
sudo systemctl restart nginx
```

Now, your web server is running, and you can upload your **static website** to /var/www/html.

Step 4: Accessing Your Personal Web Server Remotely

185

1. Accessing Locally

To access your web server locally on the same network, simply use your Raspberry Pi's IP address in the browser, e.g., `http://<RaspberryPi_IP>`.

2. Accessing Remotely (Optional)

If you want to access your Raspberry Pi's web server remotely (outside your local network), you can configure **port forwarding** on your router. This allows external traffic to access your Raspberry Pi through a specific port (usually port 80 for HTTP).

1. Log into your router's web interface.
2. Find the **port forwarding** section and forward port **80** to the Raspberry Pi's local IP address.
3. Use your **public IP address** (which you can find by searching "What is my IP?") to access your web server remotely.

Note: Exposing your Raspberry Pi to the internet can have security risks. Consider using a service like **DynDNS** or a **VPN** for secure remote access.

Final Thoughts

In this chapter, we have transformed your **Raspberry Pi** into a fully functional **web server** using **Apache** or **Nginx**. We explored how to set up a simple website or blog using **WordPress** and how to configure the server for local or remote access.

Whether you choose **Apache** or **Nginx**, both web servers provide a reliable and efficient way to host websites and applications on your Raspberry Pi. You can expand your setup by adding more features, such as **SSL encryption**, **content management systems**, or **custom web applications**. The Raspberry Pi's flexibility and low cost make it an ideal platform for learning web development and hosting personal projects.

CHAPTER 20

BUILDING A WEATHER STATION

Connecting Various Sensors (Humidity, Temperature, Barometer) to Build a Weather Station

A **weather station** is an excellent project to measure and monitor various environmental parameters such as **temperature**, **humidity**, and **air pressure**. By connecting a variety of sensors to the **Raspberry Pi**, you can create a **real-time weather station** that collects data and displays it on a web interface.

In this chapter, we'll walk through how to:

1. Connect sensors like **temperature**, **humidity**, and **barometric pressure** to the Raspberry Pi.
2. Collect and display the real-time weather data using a simple **web interface** hosted on the Raspberry Pi.

Step 1: Gathering the Necessary Components

To build your weather station, you will need the following components:

- **Raspberry Pi** (any model with GPIO support)
- **DHT22** or **DHT11** sensor (for temperature and humidity)
- **BMP180** or **BME280** sensor (for barometric pressure)
- **Jumper wires** (for connecting the sensors to the GPIO pins)
- **Breadboard** (optional, for easy connections)
- **MicroSD card** with Raspberry Pi OS installed
- **Power supply** for the Raspberry Pi
- **Python** (for coding the sensor interactions and web server)
- **Flask** (for creating the web interface)

Step 2: Wiring the Sensors to the Raspberry Pi

1. Wiring the DHT22/DHT11 Sensor (Temperature and Humidity)

The **DHT22** (or **DHT11**) is a simple and affordable sensor that can measure temperature and humidity. Here's how to connect the DHT22 to the Raspberry Pi:

1. **VCC** to **5V** (or **3.3V** depending on the sensor model) on the Raspberry Pi.
2. **GND** to **Ground**.
3. **DATA** to a **GPIO pin** (e.g., **GPIO4**) on the Raspberry Pi.

189

2. Wiring the BMP180/BME280 Sensor (Barometric Pressure)

The **BMP180** and **BME280** sensors measure atmospheric pressure, temperature, and humidity. These sensors communicate with the Raspberry Pi via **I2C**.

1. **VCC** to **3.3V** on the Raspberry Pi.
2. **GND** to **Ground**.
3. **SCL** to **SCL (GPIO3)**.
4. **SDA** to **SDA (GPIO2)**.

Ensure that the **I2C interface** is enabled on the Raspberry Pi. You can enable it by running:

```bash

sudo raspi-config
```

Then navigate to **Interface Options > I2C** and select **Enable**.

Step 3: Installing Required Libraries

To interface with the sensors and read data from them, we'll need some Python libraries:

190

1. **Install Adafruit DHT library** for the DHT sensor:

```bash

sudo pip3 install Adafruit-DHT
```

2. **Install the smbus2 and bme280 libraries** for the BMP180/BME280 sensor:

```bash

sudo pip3 install smbus2
sudo pip3 install bme280
```

3. **Install Flask** for creating a web interface:

```bash

sudo pip3 install flask
```

Step 4: Writing the Python Code to Collect Data

Now that we have our sensors connected and the necessary libraries installed, let's write the Python code that will collect the data from the sensors.

Create a new Python file (e.g., **weather_station.py**) and open it in a text editor:

```bash
bash

nano weather_station.py
```

Code for Reading the Sensors

```python
python

import time
import Adafruit_DHT
import smbus2
import bme280
from flask import Flask, render_template

# Initialize the Flask application
app = Flask(__name__)

# Initialize the DHT22 sensor
DHT_SENSOR = Adafruit_DHT.DHT22
DHT_PIN = 4

# Initialize the BME280 sensor
bus = smbus2.SMBus(1)
address = 0x76
calibration_params                              =
bme280.load_calibration_params(bus, address)

# Function to read temperature and humidity from
DHT22
def read_dht22():
```

```
    humidity,              temperature            =
Adafruit_DHT.read_retry(DHT_SENSOR, DHT_PIN)
    return temperature, humidity


# Function to read temperature, humidity, and
pressure from BME280
def read_bme280():
    bme280_data = bme280.sample(bus, address)
    temperature = bme280_data.temperature
    pressure = bme280_data.pressure
    humidity = bme280_data.humidity
    return temperature, pressure, humidity


# Route for the web interface
@app.route("/")
def index():
    # Read data from sensors
    temperature_dht, humidity_dht = read_dht22()
    temperature_bme, pressure_bme, humidity_bme
= read_bme280()


    # Prepare data to display
    data = {
        "temperature_dht":
round(temperature_dht, 2),
        "humidity_dht": round(humidity_dht, 2),
        "temperature_bme":
round(temperature_bme, 2),
        "pressure_bme": round(pressure_bme, 2),
```

```
        "humidity_bme": round(humidity_bme, 2),
    }


    return          render_template('index.html',
data=data)


# Run the web server
if __name__ == "__main__":
    app.run(host='0.0.0.0', port=80, debug=True)
```

Explanation of the Code:

1. **DHT22 Sensor**: We read the temperature and humidity from the DHT22 sensor using the `Adafruit_DHT.read_retry()` method.

2. **BME280 Sensor**: We read temperature, pressure, and humidity data from the BME280 sensor using the `bme280.sample()` method.

3. **Flask Web Application**: We use Flask to create a simple web interface that displays the data from both sensors. The `render_template()` function passes the sensor data to an **HTML template** for display.

Step 5: Creating the Web Interface (HTML Template)

Now, let's create the **HTML template** to display the data in a readable format. Create a folder called **templates** in the same directory as your Python script and inside it, create a file named **index.html**.

bash

```
mkdir templates
nano templates/index.html
```

Add the following HTML code to the file:

html

```
<!DOCTYPE html>
<html lang="en">
<head>
    <meta charset="UTF-8">
    <meta name="viewport" content="width=device-width, initial-scale=1.0">
    <title>Weather Station</title>
</head>
<body>
    <h1>Weather Station</h1>
    <p><strong>Temperature (DHT22):</strong> {{ data.temperature_dht }} &#8451;</p>
    <p><strong>Humidity (DHT22):</strong> {{ data.humidity_dht }} %</p>
```

```
    <p><strong>Temperature (BME280):</strong> {{
data.temperature_bme }} &#8451;</p>
    <p><strong>Pressure   (BME280):</strong>   {{
data.pressure_bme }} hPa</p>
    <p><strong>Humidity   (BME280):</strong>   {{
data.humidity_bme }} %</p>
</body>
</html>
```

Explanation of the HTML Code:

- We display the temperature, humidity, and pressure data in a simple format using **Flask's Jinja templating engine**. The values from the Python script are passed to this template via the `data` dictionary.

Step 6: Running the Weather Station

1. Save the Python script and HTML template.
2. Run the Python script:

```bash
bash
```

```
python3 weather_station.py
```

3. Open a browser and go to `http://<RaspberryPi_IP>` to view your weather

196

station interface. You should see real-time data from the sensors displayed on the web page.

Step 7: Accessing the Weather Station Remotely

To access your weather station remotely, you can set up **port forwarding** on your router. Forward port **80** (HTTP) to the Raspberry Pi's IP address, so you can access the web interface from any device in your network by using your public IP address.

Final Thoughts

In this chapter, we built a **weather station** using the Raspberry Pi and a set of sensors to collect **temperature**, **humidity**, and **barometric pressure** data. We used **Flask** to create a web interface that displays the real-time data from the sensors. This project is a great starting point for building more advanced environmental monitoring systems.

You can expand this weather station project by:

- Adding additional sensors (e.g., wind speed, rainfall).

197

- Storing the data in a database like **SQLite** for long-term tracking.
- Visualizing the data with graphs using tools like **Matplotlib** or **Plotly**.
- Integrating cloud services to store and analyze the data remotely.

With the Raspberry Pi as the core of your weather station, you have endless possibilities for customization and expansion!

CHAPTER 21

SMART GARAGE DOOR OPENER

Building a Smart Garage Door Opener with Raspberry Pi

A **Smart Garage Door Opener** is a perfect project to integrate the **Raspberry Pi** into your home automation system. By using a Raspberry Pi, you can control your garage door remotely through a mobile app, **Bluetooth**, or **Wi-Fi**. This project will give you the ability to open and close your garage door from anywhere, increasing convenience and security.

In this chapter, we will:

1. Build a **smart garage door opener** using a Raspberry Pi.
2. Set up **Bluetooth** or **Wi-Fi** for remote control of the garage door.

Step 1: Components Needed

To create a smart garage door opener, you will need the following components:

- **Raspberry Pi** (any model with GPIO support)
- **Relay Module** (to control the garage door motor)
- **Magnetic Reed Switch** (to detect whether the door is open or closed)
- **Bluetooth or Wi-Fi Module** (depending on your remote control preference)
- **Jumper wires** and **Breadboard**
- **MicroSD card** with Raspberry Pi OS installed
- **Power supply** for the Raspberry Pi
- **Garage door opener motor** (that can be controlled via a relay)
- **Mobile phone or computer** (to control the door via Bluetooth or Wi-Fi)

Step 2: Wiring the Relay and Sensors

1. Connecting the Relay to the Garage Door Motor

The **Relay Module** will be used to control the garage door motor. The Raspberry Pi will send signals to the relay, which will open or close the garage door.

1. **Relay Module**:
   - **VCC** to **5V** on the Raspberry Pi.
   - **GND** to **Ground**.

- o **IN** to a **GPIO pin** (e.g., **GPIO17**) on the Raspberry Pi.

2. **Garage Door Motor**:

- o Connect the **garage door motor's control wires** to the relay's **Common (COM)** and **Normally Open (NO)** terminals. When the relay is triggered, it will complete the circuit and activate the motor.

2. Adding the Magnetic Reed Switch (Door Position Sensor)

A **Magnetic Reed Switch** detects whether the garage door is open or closed by sensing the position of a magnet attached to the door.

1. **Reed Switch**:

- o **One terminal** to **GPIO pin** (e.g., **GPIO18**) on the Raspberry Pi.
- o **Other terminal** to **Ground**.

When the garage door is closed, the reed switch will be **closed** (connected), and when the door is open, the switch will be **open** (disconnected).

Step 3: Setting Up Remote Control Using Bluetooth or Wi-Fi

1. Bluetooth Control (Using Bluetooth Low Energy)

Bluetooth allows you to control the garage door with your smartphone or a Bluetooth-enabled device. The Raspberry Pi will act as a Bluetooth server and listen for commands.

Installing the Bluetooth Packages on Raspberry Pi:

1. Install the necessary Bluetooth packages on your Raspberry Pi:

    ```bash
    sudo apt-get update
    sudo apt-get install pi-bluetooth bluez
    sudo systemctl enable bluetooth
    ```

2. Make sure **Bluetooth** is enabled on your Raspberry Pi by checking the **Bluetooth settings**.

Creating a Python Script to Control the Garage Door via Bluetooth:

You will need to create a Python script that communicates with the Bluetooth service and opens or closes the door when commands are received.

1. Import the required libraries:

```python
import RPi.GPIO as GPIO
import time
import bluetooth
```

2. Set up the GPIO and Bluetooth communication:

```python
GPIO.setmode(GPIO.BCM)
relay_pin = 17  # Relay to control the motor
reed_switch_pin = 18  # Reed switch for door status
GPIO.setup(relay_pin, GPIO.OUT)
GPIO.setup(reed_switch_pin,      GPIO.IN,
pull_up_down=GPIO.PUD_UP)

# Bluetooth server address and port
```

```
server_sock                         =
bluetooth.BluetoothSocket(bluetooth.RFCOM
M)
server_sock.bind(("", bluetooth.PORT_ANY))
server_sock.listen(1)
print("Waiting        for        Bluetooth
connection...")


client_sock,         client_info         =
server_sock.accept()
print("Accepted      connection      from",
client_info)
```

3. Check for commands and control the door:

```python
while True:
    data = client_sock.recv(1024)
    if data == b'open':
        GPIO.output(relay_pin, GPIO.HIGH)
# Open the door
        print("Door is opening...")
        time.sleep(5)  # Keep the door open
for 5 seconds
        GPIO.output(relay_pin, GPIO.LOW)
# Stop the motor
    elif data == b'close':
        GPIO.output(relay_pin, GPIO.HIGH)
# Close the door
```

```
        print("Door is closing...")
        time.sleep(5)    # Keep the door
closed for 5 seconds
        GPIO.output(relay_pin,    GPIO.LOW)
# Stop the motor
```

4. To connect the Bluetooth device, use any Bluetooth-enabled phone and pair it with the Raspberry Pi. Once connected, send the command open or close via a Bluetooth app to control the garage door.

2. Wi-Fi Control (Using Flask Web Server)

Wi-Fi allows you to control the garage door from anywhere in your home or remotely via the internet. The **Flask** web framework will enable us to create a simple web interface for controlling the garage door.

Setting Up a Flask Web Server on Raspberry Pi:

1. Install Flask:

   ```bash
   bash
   ```

   ```bash
   sudo pip3 install flask
   ```

2. Create a Python script to run the web server:

```python
python

from flask import Flask
import RPi.GPIO as GPIO
import time

app = Flask(__name__)

GPIO.setmode(GPIO.BCM)
relay_pin = 17
reed_switch_pin = 18
GPIO.setup(relay_pin, GPIO.OUT)
GPIO.setup(reed_switch_pin,          GPIO.IN,
pull_up_down=GPIO.PUD_UP)

@app.route("/open")
def open_door():
    GPIO.output(relay_pin, GPIO.HIGH)
    print("Door is opening...")
    time.sleep(5)
    GPIO.output(relay_pin, GPIO.LOW)
    return "Garage door is opening!"

@app.route("/close")
def close_door():
    GPIO.output(relay_pin, GPIO.HIGH)
    print("Door is closing...")
    time.sleep(5)
    GPIO.output(relay_pin, GPIO.LOW)
```

```
      return "Garage door is closing!"


@app.route("/status")
def door_status():
    if  GPIO.input(reed_switch_pin)  ==
GPIO.HIGH:
        return "Garage door is open."
    else:
        return "Garage door is closed."


if __name__ == "__main__":
    app.run(host='0.0.0.0', port=80)
```

3. Run the Flask app:

```bash
```

```
python3 garage_door.py
```

4. Open a web browser and go to `http://<RaspberryPi_IP>/open` to open the garage door or `http://<RaspberryPi_IP>/close` to close it. You can also check the door's status by visiting `http://<RaspberryPi_IP>/status`.

Step 4: Adding Security Features

To improve the security of your smart garage door opener, you can add a few additional features:

- **Password Protection**: Implement basic authentication on the web server to prevent unauthorized access.
- **Bluetooth Pairing**: Ensure the Bluetooth app is paired with the Raspberry Pi before allowing control, adding an extra layer of security.
- **Motion Sensors**: Add motion sensors to automatically close the door after a period of inactivity or if the door remains open for too long.

Final Thoughts

In this chapter, we have created a **smart garage door opener** using a **Raspberry Pi**, a **relay module**, and either **Bluetooth** or **Wi-Fi** for remote control. The Raspberry Pi serves as the central controller, allowing you to open and close the garage door from anywhere via a mobile app or a web interface.

This project is an excellent way to integrate **home automation** into your everyday life. You can expand it by adding features like **voice control**, **automated scheduling**, or **motion sensors** for added convenience and security. With the Raspberry Pi, the possibilities for smart home projects are limitless!

CHAPTER 22

RASPBERRY PI FOR GAMING

Setting up Raspberry Pi as a Retro Gaming Console Using RetroPie

The **Raspberry Pi** is an excellent platform for retro gaming. Thanks to its low cost and flexibility, it can be transformed into a **retro gaming console** that plays classic games from consoles like the **NES**, **SNES**, **Genesis**, **PlayStation**, and more. With the help of **RetroPie**, a popular emulator platform for the Raspberry Pi, you can easily recreate the experience of playing these vintage games on modern hardware.

In this chapter, we'll guide you through:

1. Setting up **RetroPie** on your Raspberry Pi.
2. Installing emulators for various gaming consoles.
3. Playing classic games on your Raspberry Pi.

Step 1: Installing RetroPie on Raspberry Pi

RetroPie is a software package that allows you to run emulators for classic gaming consoles on your Raspberry Pi.

210

It combines several emulators into one interface, making it easy to manage and play your favorite games.

1. Download and Install RetroPie

1. **Download RetroPie**:
   o Visit the RetroPie website and download the latest **RetroPie** image for your Raspberry Pi model (e.g., Raspberry Pi 4, 3, or Zero).
2. **Write the Image to an SD Card**:
   o Use the **Raspberry Pi Imager** or **Etcher** to write the RetroPie image to a **microSD card** (at least 8GB recommended).
   o Insert the microSD card into your Raspberry Pi.
3. **First Boot**:
   o Insert the **microSD card** into your Raspberry Pi, connect it to a monitor or TV, and power it on.
   o RetroPie will automatically boot up and guide you through some basic setup steps, including configuring your controller.

Step 2: Configuring Controllers

To play retro games, you need a controller. RetroPie supports a wide variety of controllers, including USB gamepads, Bluetooth controllers, and even keyboards.

1. Configure USB Controllers

1. When RetroPie first boots up, it will prompt you to configure a controller.
2. Follow the on-screen instructions to map the buttons on your controller (e.g., arrow keys, A, B, X, Y, etc.).
3. After the initial configuration, you can use your controller to navigate RetroPie's interface.

2. Configure Bluetooth Controllers

To use a **Bluetooth controller** (e.g., PlayStation, Xbox, or third-party Bluetooth controllers), follow these steps:

1. From the **RetroPie main menu**, navigate to **RetroPie Settings > Bluetooth**.
2. Select **Register and Connect to Bluetooth Device**.
3. Follow the prompts to connect your Bluetooth controller to the Raspberry Pi.

Once connected, you can use the Bluetooth controller to play games.

Step 3: Installing Emulators

RetroPie comes pre-installed with a variety of **emulators** for different gaming consoles. These emulators allow you to play classic games on your Raspberry Pi.

1. Installing Additional Emulators

RetroPie automatically installs many popular emulators, but you can also add more by following these steps:

1. From the **RetroPie main menu**, go to **RetroPie Settings**.
2. Select **Manage Packages** > **Optional Packages**.
3. Here, you'll find a list of emulators that are not pre-installed. Select the ones you want to install (e.g., **PS1**, **Game Boy Advance**, **Genesis**).

Each emulator has different setup requirements, but RetroPie's interface makes it easy to install and configure them.

Step 4: Adding ROMs (Games)

To play games on RetroPie, you'll need **ROMs** (game files). RetroPie doesn't come with games, so you'll need to source ROMs from a legal source (you can dump ROMs from your own physical games if you own them).

1. Adding ROMs via USB Drive

1. Format a **USB flash drive** to **FAT32**.
2. Create a folder named **retropie** on the USB drive.
3. Insert the USB drive into your Raspberry Pi and wait for RetroPie to automatically create the necessary directories.
4. After RetroPie finishes, remove the USB drive and connect it to your computer.
5. Inside the **retropie/roms** directory, you'll see subfolders for each emulator (e.g., **nes**, **snes**, **genesis**).
6. your ROMs into the corresponding emulator folder on the USB drive.
7. Insert the USB drive back into the Raspberry Pi. RetroPie will automatically the ROMs into the correct locations.

2. Adding ROMs via Network Share (Wi-Fi)

If your Raspberry Pi is connected to the network via Wi-Fi or Ethernet, you can transfer ROMs using a network share.

214

1. On your Raspberry Pi, navigate to **RetroPie** > **Raspberry Pi Settings** > **Network** > **Wi-Fi** and connect to your Wi-Fi network.

2. On your computer, open the file manager and type `\\<RaspberryPi_IP>` (replace `<RaspberryPi_IP>` with your actual Raspberry Pi IP address).

3. Access the **roms** folder and your ROMs into the appropriate emulator folders.

Step 5: Playing Games on Your Raspberry Pi

Once you've installed RetroPie, configured your controller, and added ROMs, you can start playing games!

1. Navigating the RetroPie Interface

1. From the RetroPie menu, navigate using your controller to the game console of your choice (e.g., **NES**, **SNES**, **PS1**).

2. Select the console, and you'll see a list of available games (ROMs) you've added.

3. Use your controller to select a game and press **A** to start playing.

2. Configuring Game Settings

You can adjust various settings for each game, including video, audio, and controls, by pressing **Start** during gameplay to access the RetroPie menu.

Step 6: Expanding Your Gaming Experience

RetroPie allows for a wide variety of customizations and additions, enabling you to enhance your retro gaming experience.

1. Save States and Load States

Most emulators on RetroPie support **save states** and **load states**, which allow you to save your progress at any point and return to it later.

- To save your game state, press **Select + R2**.
- To load your game state, press **Select + L2**.

2. Adding Cheats

RetroPie supports cheats for many emulators. You can activate cheats by editing the **cheat codes** file for a specific emulator. For example, for the **SNES**, you can enable infinite lives, unlock all levels, and other fun cheat features.

3. Multiplayer Gaming

If you want to play **multiplayer** games, RetroPie supports local multiplayer for many consoles. Simply connect additional controllers (either USB or Bluetooth) and select **Player 2**, **Player 3**, etc., when starting the game.

Final Thoughts

In this chapter, we've transformed your **Raspberry Pi** into a **retro gaming console** using **RetroPie**. Whether you want to relive classic **NES**, **SNES**, **PlayStation**, or **Genesis** games, RetroPie provides an all-in-one solution to play a wide range of retro games. With support for multiple emulators, easy ROM management, and controller configuration, it's an excellent project for anyone who enjoys gaming and homebrew projects.

You can expand your setup by:

- Adding **Bluetooth controllers** for wireless gaming.

- Using **external storage** or **network shares** to increase your ROM collection.
- Setting up **RetroPie themes** to customize the appearance of the interface.
- Exploring **advanced emulation options** for systems like **arcade machines** (MAME), **Atari**, and more.

RetroPie is a fun and versatile platform that turns your Raspberry Pi into a powerful retro gaming machine with minimal setup. Enjoy playing your favorite classic games right on your Raspberry Pi!

CHAPTER 23

SMART GARDENING SYSTEM

Creating a System to Monitor and Control Soil Moisture, Light, and Temperature for Plants

Gardening doesn't have to be limited to the outdoors anymore. With the help of the **Raspberry Pi**, you can build a **smart gardening system** that monitors and controls key environmental factors for plants, such as **soil moisture**, **light**, and **temperature**. This can help you grow healthier plants by automating processes like watering, lighting, and temperature regulation, while also giving you real-time data about your plants' environment.

In this chapter, we will walk through:

1. Building a **smart gardening system** that monitors soil moisture, temperature, and light levels.
2. Implementing an **automatic watering system** based on soil moisture levels.

Step 1: Components Needed

To create your smart gardening system, you will need the following components:

- **Raspberry Pi** (any model with GPIO support)
- **DHT22** (or DHT11) sensor (for temperature and humidity)
- **Soil Moisture Sensor**
- **Light Sensor** (e.g., **LDR** - Light Dependent Resistor)
- **Relay Module** (to control the water pump)
- **Water Pump** (for the automatic watering system)
- **Jumper wires**
- **Breadboard** (optional, for easy connections)
- **Power supply** for the Raspberry Pi
- **MicroSD card** with Raspberry Pi OS installed
- **Python** (for coding the system)
- **Flask** (for displaying data on a web interface)

Step 2: Wiring the Sensors and Watering System

1. Connecting the Soil Moisture Sensor

The **soil moisture sensor** detects the water content in the soil. When the soil becomes dry, the sensor will trigger the watering system.

1. **VCC** to **5V** (or **3.3V** depending on the sensor).
2. **GND** to **Ground**.
3. **A0** (Analog Pin) to an **ADC pin** (if using analog sensors) or **GPIO pin** (if using a digital sensor) on the Raspberry Pi (e.g., **GPIO17**).

2. Connecting the DHT22 Sensor (Temperature and Humidity)

The **DHT22** sensor is used to monitor the temperature and humidity of the environment around your plants.

1. **VCC** to **3.3V** on the Raspberry Pi.
2. **GND** to **Ground**.
3. **DATA** to **GPIO4** (or any other GPIO pin).

3. Connecting the Light Sensor (LDR)

The **Light Dependent Resistor (LDR)** measures light intensity. The resistance of the LDR decreases with increased light, which can be measured by the Raspberry Pi.

1. One terminal of the LDR connects to **3.3V**.
2. The other terminal connects to **GPIO18** and also to a **10kΩ resistor** that connects to **Ground**.

4. Setting up the Water Pump with Relay

To automate watering, you can use a **relay module** to control a small water pump.

1. **Relay VCC** to **5V** on the Raspberry Pi.
2. **Relay GND** to **Ground**.
3. **Relay IN** to a **GPIO pin** (e.g., **GPIO23**) on the Raspberry Pi.
4. Connect the **water pump** to the **relay's Common (COM)** and **Normally Open (NO)** terminals. The water pump will activate when the relay is triggered.

Step 3: Writing the Python Code to Monitor and Control the System

We will write Python code to:

1. Read data from the **soil moisture**, **light**, and **temperature** sensors.
2. Trigger the **water pump** based on the soil moisture levels.
3. Display the real-time data on a **web interface** using **Flask**.

1. Installing the Necessary Libraries

First, install the required libraries for sensor communication and Flask:

```bash
bash
```

```bash
sudo pip3 install Adafruit_DHT flask RPi.GPIO
```

- **Adafruit_DHT** is the library to communicate with the DHT22 sensor.
- **RPi.GPIO** is for controlling the GPIO pins on the Raspberry Pi.
- **Flask** is for creating a simple web interface.

2. Writing the Python Code

Create a new Python script (`smart_garden.py`):

```bash
bash
```

```bash
nano smart_garden.py
```

Add the following code:

```python
python
```

```python
import RPi.GPIO as GPIO
import time
```

223

```python
import Adafruit_DHT
from flask import Flask, render_template

# Set up Flask app
app = Flask(__name__)

# Set up GPIO
GPIO.setmode(GPIO.BCM)
moisture_sensor_pin = 17   # GPIO pin for soil
moisture sensor
light_sensor_pin = 18     # GPIO pin for light
sensor (LDR)
relay_pin = 23            # GPIO pin for controlling
water pump

# Set up relay to control the water pump
GPIO.setup(relay_pin, GPIO.OUT)

# Set up soil moisture sensor (digital)
GPIO.setup(moisture_sensor_pin, GPIO.IN)

# Set up light sensor (LDR)
GPIO.setup(light_sensor_pin, GPIO.IN)

# Set up DHT22 sensor for temperature and
humidity
DHT_SENSOR = Adafruit_DHT.DHT22
DHT_PIN = 4  # GPIO pin where DHT22 data pin is
connected
```

```python
# Function to read soil moisture
def read_soil_moisture():
    if GPIO.input(moisture_sensor_pin) == GPIO.HIGH:
        return "Dry"
    else:
        return "Wet"

# Function to read temperature and humidity
def read_temperature_humidity():
    humidity, temperature = Adafruit_DHT.read_retry(DHT_SENSOR, DHT_PIN)
    return round(temperature, 2), round(humidity, 2)

# Function to read light intensity
def read_light_intensity():
    return GPIO.input(light_sensor_pin)

# Function to control watering system
def water_plants():
    GPIO.output(relay_pin, GPIO.HIGH)  # Turn on water pump
    time.sleep(5)  # Water for 5 seconds
    GPIO.output(relay_pin, GPIO.LOW)  # Turn off water pump

# Web interface to show data and control system
```

```python
@app.route("/")
def index():
    # Get data from sensors
    moisture = read_soil_moisture()
    temperature, humidity = read_temperature_humidity()
    light = read_light_intensity()

    # Check soil moisture and water the plants if dry
    if moisture == "Dry":
        water_plants()

    # Prepare data to display on the web page
    data = {
        "moisture": moisture,
        "temperature": temperature,
        "humidity": humidity,
        "light": "Low" if light == GPIO.LOW else "High"
    }

    return render_template("index.html", data=data)

# Run the Flask app
if __name__ == "__main__":
    app.run(host='0.0.0.0', port=80, debug=True)
```

226

Explanation of the Code:

- **Soil Moisture**: The **read_soil_moisture()** function checks the moisture sensor. If the soil is dry, it will activate the watering system.
- **Temperature and Humidity**: The **read_temperature_humidity()** function reads data from the DHT22 sensor.
- **Light**: The **read_light_intensity()** function checks the light sensor to determine whether the plant has enough light.
- **Watering System**: The **water_plants()** function activates the relay to turn on the water pump for 5 seconds, simulating an automatic watering system.
- **Web Interface**: The Flask app runs a web server that displays real-time sensor data (moisture, temperature, humidity, and light levels).

Step 4: Creating the Web Interface (HTML Template)

Create a folder named **templates** in the same directory as the Python script, and inside that folder, create a file called **index.html**:

```bash
mkdir templates
nano templates/index.html
```

Add the following HTML code to display the sensor data:

```html
<!DOCTYPE html>
<html lang="en">
<head>
    <meta charset="UTF-8">
    <meta name="viewport" content="width=device-width, initial-scale=1.0">
    <title>Smart Gardening System</title>
</head>
<body>
    <h1>Smart Gardening System</h1>
    <p><strong>Soil     Moisture:</strong>     {{ data.moisture }}</p>
    <p><strong>Temperature:</strong>           {{ data.temperature }} &#8451;</p>
    <p><strong>Humidity:</strong>              {{ data.humidity }} %</p>
    <p><strong>Light    Intensity:</strong>    {{ data.light }}</p>

    <h2>System Status:</h2>
```

```
<p>Watering system is running if soil is
dry.</p>
</body>
</html>
```

Explanation of the HTML Code:

- The data from the Python script (moisture, temperature, humidity, and light) is passed to the HTML template using Flask's Jinja templating engine.

Step 5: Running the Smart Gardening System

1. Save the Python script and HTML template.
2. Run the Python script:

```bash

python3 smart_garden.py
```

3. Open a browser and navigate to `http://<RaspberryPi_IP>` to view your gardening system interface. You will see the real-time data from your sensors, and the system will automatically water the plants if the soil is dry.

Step 6: Expanding Your Smart Gardening System

To enhance your smart gardening system, consider adding the following features:

- **Automatic Light Control**: Integrate a smart light control system to ensure your plants receive optimal light levels.
- **Data Logging**: Store sensor data in a database like **SQLite** for long-term monitoring and analysis.
- **Mobile Notifications**: Integrate with **Pushbullet** or **Twilio** to send notifications to your phone when the system waters the plants or if conditions change.
- **Cloud Integration**: Store your gardening data on the cloud (e.g., **Google Sheets**, **AWS**, or **ThingSpeak**) for remote monitoring and analysis.

Final Thoughts

In this chapter, we built a **smart gardening system** that monitors key environmental factors such as **soil moisture**, **light**, and **temperature**. The system uses a **soil moisture sensor** to trigger automatic watering and displays the data on a **Flask web interface**.

This project is a great way to combine **IoT** and **automation** to take care of your plants and can be expanded with additional features to make it even more sophisticated. With the Raspberry Pi, you can create a fully automated, real-time gardening system that can keep your plants healthy with minimal effort.

CHAPTER 24

RASPBERRY PI AND AI

Introduction to Artificial Intelligence and Machine Learning with Raspberry Pi

The **Raspberry Pi** is an excellent platform for exploring **Artificial Intelligence (AI)** and **Machine Learning (ML)** due to its low cost, versatility, and ease of use. With the power of Python libraries and the growing number of AI frameworks available for the Raspberry Pi, you can start experimenting with various AI concepts right away.

In this chapter, we'll explore how you can use the Raspberry Pi for AI and machine learning tasks. Specifically, we'll focus on setting up a **facial recognition system** using the **OpenCV** library, one of the most popular computer vision libraries.

Step 1: Understanding AI and Machine Learning on Raspberry Pi

AI and ML refer to the development of systems that can "learn" from data to make decisions or predictions. While **AI** encompasses a broad range of intelligent behaviors, **machine learning** (a subset of AI) is specifically concerned with algorithms that improve their performance as they are exposed to more data.

On the Raspberry Pi, you can run AI and ML models that can perform tasks like:

- **Object recognition** (e.g., facial recognition, object detection).
- **Speech recognition** (e.g., voice control systems).
- **Predictive analytics** (e.g., forecasting stock prices, weather predictions).
- **Natural language processing** (e.g., chatbots, sentiment analysis).

The Raspberry Pi's **ARM processor** is powerful enough to handle basic AI tasks, especially when combined with libraries like **TensorFlow Lite**, **OpenCV**, and **scikit-learn**. While it may not be as powerful as specialized AI hardware, it's more than capable for many home automation and DIY AI projects.

233

Step 2: Setting Up the Raspberry Pi for AI Projects

Before diving into machine learning, let's first set up your Raspberry Pi with the necessary tools:

1. Install Raspberry Pi OS

Ensure that you have **Raspberry Pi OS** installed on your Raspberry Pi. If you haven't done this already, you can install it using the **Raspberry Pi Imager**.

2. Update the Raspberry Pi

Once Raspberry Pi OS is installed, open the terminal and run the following commands to update the software:

```bash

sudo apt-get update
sudo apt-get upgrade
```

3. Install Dependencies for AI and ML

We'll use **OpenCV** for computer vision tasks like facial recognition. Install OpenCV by running:

```bash

```

234

```
sudo apt-get install python3-opencv
```

For machine learning tasks, **scikit-learn** and **TensorFlow Lite** are also useful libraries. Install them as follows:

```
bash
```

```
sudo pip3 install scikit-learn
sudo pip3 install tflite-runtime
```

Step 3: Setting Up a Basic Facial Recognition System

Facial recognition is a practical AI application that can be implemented on the Raspberry Pi. It's widely used for security systems, home automation, and even personalized user experiences. We will use **OpenCV**, a powerful computer vision library, to implement facial recognition.

1. Install Required Libraries

In addition to OpenCV, you need the **dlib** library, which provides tools for facial detection and recognition. Install dlib by running the following command:

```
bash
```

```
sudo apt-get install python3-dlib
```

2. Python Code for Facial Recognition

Let's write a Python script that detects faces using OpenCV and recognizes them.

1. **Set up the camera**: The **Raspberry Pi Camera Module** or a **USB webcam** can be used for this project. Ensure that the camera is connected and enabled by running:

   ```bash
   sudo raspi-config
   ```

   Navigate to **Interface Options** > **Camera** and enable it.

2. **Create the Python Script**: Open a new Python file (`face_recognition.py`):

   ```bash
   nano face_recognition.py
   ```

3. **Write the Code**:

```python
```

```
import cv2
import dlib
import numpy as np

# Initialize the webcam
cap = cv2.VideoCapture(0)

# Initialize the face detector
detector = dlib.get_frontal_face_detector()

# Initialize the facial landmarks predictor
predictor                             =
dlib.shape_predictor('shape_predictor_68_face_l
andmarks.dat')

# Load the face recognition model
recognizer                            =
dlib.face_recognition_model_v1('dlib_face_recog
nition_resnet_model_v1.dat')

# Store face encodings for known faces
known_face_encodings = []
known_face_names = []

# Function to encode faces
def encode_faces(frame):
    gray         =        cv2.cvtColor(frame,
cv2.COLOR_BGR2GRAY)
```

237

```
    faces = detector(gray)
    face_encodings = []

    for face in faces:
        landmarks = predictor(gray, face)
        encoding                        =
recognizer.compute_face_descriptor(frame,
landmarks)

face_encodings.append(np.array(encoding))

    return face_encodings, faces

# Start video capture
while True:
    ret, frame = cap.read()
    if not ret:
        break

    # Get face encodings and locations
    face_encodings, faces = encode_faces(frame)

    # Loop through each face found
    for i, face in enumerate(faces):
        (x, y, w, h) = (face.left(), face.top(),
face.width(), face.height())

        # Draw a rectangle around the face
```

```
        cv2.rectangle(frame, (x, y), (x + w, y +
h), (0, 255, 0), 2)


        # Compare the face encoding with known
encodings
        matches = []
        for        known_encoding        in
known_face_encodings:
            match                          =
np.linalg.norm(known_encoding              -
face_encodings[i])
            matches.append(match)


        if matches:
            # The smallest distance means a match
            best_match_index               =
np.argmin(matches)
            name                           =
known_face_names[best_match_index]
        else:
            name = "Unknown"


        # Display the name
        cv2.putText(frame, name, (x, y - 10),
cv2.FONT_HERSHEY_SIMPLEX, 0.9, (255, 255, 255),
2)


    # Display the resulting frame
    cv2.imshow("Face Recognition", frame)
```

239

```
# Exit on pressing 'q'
if cv2.waitKey(1) & 0xFF == ord('q'):
    break
```

```
# Release the webcam and close the window
cap.release()
cv2.destroyAllWindows()
```

Explanation of the Code:

- **dlib.get_frontal_face_detector()**: Detects faces in the video stream.
- **dlib.shape_predictor()**: This is used to detect the landmarks on the face.
- **dlib.face_recognition_model_v1**: Computes a vector (encoding) representing the face, which can be compared to stored encodings for identification.
- **Video Capture**: Captures the webcam feed and processes each frame.
- **Face Detection and Recognition**: Detects faces, computes encodings, and compares them to known faces to display a name.

3. Running the Facial Recognition System

To run the system, save the script and execute it:

bash

240

```
python3 face_recognition.py
```

When you run this script, your Raspberry Pi will start capturing video, detect faces, and display the name of recognized faces based on the stored encodings.

Step 4: Expanding the System

You can expand the facial recognition system by adding more features:

- **Face Registration**: You can add a feature to register new faces by capturing the encoding and storing it with the corresponding name.
- **Real-time Notifications**: Integrate email or SMS alerts using services like **Twilio** to notify you when a new face is detected.
- **Integration with Home Automation**: Use the recognized face data to trigger actions such as opening a door or controlling smart home devices.

Final Thoughts

In this chapter, we've introduced the basics of **artificial intelligence** and **machine learning** using the **Raspberry Pi**. We focused on **facial recognition**, a practical and fun application of AI, and used **OpenCV** and **dlib** to create a simple facial recognition system. This system can be expanded for various applications, from security to automation.

AI on the Raspberry Pi opens up a world of possibilities, from **voice assistants** to **object detection** and beyond. The Raspberry Pi is a powerful tool for learning and experimenting with AI, making it an ideal platform for home projects and educational purposes.

CHAPTER 25

RASPBERRY PI FOR EDUCATION

Using Raspberry Pi as an Educational Tool in Schools and Workshops

The **Raspberry Pi** is more than just a powerful single-board computer; it's an excellent educational tool that can be used to teach a wide variety of subjects, from programming and electronics to robotics and data science. With its low cost, open-source nature, and community-driven resources, the Raspberry Pi has become a popular choice for educators in schools and workshops around the world.

In this chapter, we'll explore:

1. How the Raspberry Pi can be used as an educational tool in schools and workshops.
2. Real-world examples of using Raspberry Pi for interactive science experiments and teaching programming.

Step 1: Why Raspberry Pi is Perfect for Education

The **Raspberry Pi** has many features that make it a great fit for teaching and learning:

- **Affordability**: At a low cost, the Raspberry Pi is an affordable tool for schools and workshops, allowing more students to access hands-on learning.
- **Flexibility**: With its ability to run multiple operating systems, software, and programming languages, it can support a wide variety of educational projects.
- **Community Support**: The large online community provides resources, lesson plans, tutorials, and shared projects for educators and students.
- **Hands-on Learning**: The Raspberry Pi encourages practical learning through hardware and software integration, making it easier for students to engage in interactive learning experiences.

Using Raspberry Pi in education encourages students to experiment, problem-solve, and think creatively, skills that are vital in today's technological world.

Step 2: Using Raspberry Pi in Schools and Workshops

The Raspberry Pi can be used in various educational settings, from classroom learning to extracurricular workshops. Here are some ideas for incorporating the Raspberry Pi into your educational activities:

1. Teaching Programming

Raspberry Pi offers a fantastic environment for learning programming. Students can start learning programming with simple tools and gradually move to more advanced projects.

- **Scratch**: A visual programming language that introduces young students to coding concepts. Scratch is perfect for beginners, allowing students to create simple games and animations.
- **Python**: The Raspberry Pi comes with **Python** pre-installed, a popular programming language for learning coding. Python is widely used in industry and education, making it a great choice for teaching.
- **Blockly**: A graphical programming language similar to Scratch, but more suited for teaching coding logic. It's a good intermediate step before diving into text-based languages.

2. Building Interactive Science Experiments

One of the most exciting ways to use the Raspberry Pi in education is by building interactive science experiments. Raspberry Pi can be used to gather data from sensors, display results in real time, and control experiments via programming.

Example: Temperature and Humidity Monitoring System

1. **Objective**: Teach students about environmental science and data collection by creating a system that monitors temperature and humidity.

2. **Components Needed**:
   o Raspberry Pi (any model with GPIO support)
   o **DHT22** or **DHT11** sensor (for temperature and humidity)
   o Jumper wires and a breadboard

3. **Setup**:
   o Connect the **DHT22** sensor to the Raspberry Pi to measure temperature and humidity.
   o Use Python and the **Adafruit DHT library** to read data from the sensor.
   o Display the data on a web interface using **Flask**.

4. **Code**: Write a simple Python script to read the temperature and humidity from the sensor and display it in real-time.

Example code to read sensor data:

```python
python

import Adafruit_DHT
import time

# Set the sensor type and the GPIO pin
sensor = Adafruit_DHT.DHT22
pin = 4

while True:
    # Read the humidity and temperature from the
sensor
    humidity,           temperature           =
Adafruit_DHT.read_retry(sensor, pin)

    if humidity is not None and temperature is
not None:
        print(f'Temperature:
{temperature:.2f}°C, Humidity: {humidity:.2f}%')
    else:
        print('Failed  to  get  data  from  the
sensor. Retrying...')
```

247

```
time.sleep(2)
```

This experiment teaches students how to interface with sensors, work with real-time data, and write Python code to automate data collection.

Step 3: Teaching Robotics with Raspberry Pi

Robotics is a powerful way to engage students in engineering, programming, and problem-solving. With the Raspberry Pi, students can build and program simple robots to perform various tasks.

Example: Building a Simple Robot

1. **Objective**: Teach students about mechanics, electronics, and programming by building a simple robot that moves based on sensor inputs.

2. **Components Needed**:
   - Raspberry Pi
   - Motors and motor driver (e.g., L298N motor driver)
   - **Ultrasonic sensor** (for distance measurement)
   - Servo motor (for robotic arm or movement control)

o   Jumper wires and breadboard

3. **Setup**:

   o   Connect the **ultrasonic sensor** to the Raspberry Pi to measure the distance to objects.

   o   Use Python to control the motors based on the distance data collected from the sensor.

   o   Program the robot to stop or avoid obstacles by reading the sensor's data.

4. **Code**: Write a Python script to control the robot's movement.

Example code for controlling motors:

```python
import RPi.GPIO as GPIO
import time

# Motor pins
motor1A = 17
motor1B = 18
motor2A = 22
motor2B = 23

# Setup
GPIO.setmode(GPIO.BCM)
GPIO.setup(motor1A, GPIO.OUT)
GPIO.setup(motor1B, GPIO.OUT)
```

```
GPIO.setup(motor2A, GPIO.OUT)
GPIO.setup(motor2B, GPIO.OUT)

# Move forward
GPIO.output(motor1A, GPIO.HIGH)
GPIO.output(motor1B, GPIO.LOW)
GPIO.output(motor2A, GPIO.HIGH)
GPIO.output(motor2B, GPIO.LOW)

time.sleep(2)

# Stop
GPIO.output(motor1A, GPIO.LOW)
GPIO.output(motor1B, GPIO.LOW)
GPIO.output(motor2A, GPIO.LOW)
GPIO.output(motor2B, GPIO.LOW)

GPIO.cleanup()
```

This experiment teaches students about **sensors**, **motors**, and **robotic control**, and introduces them to **hardware programming** with the Raspberry Pi.

Step 4: Incorporating Raspberry Pi into Classroom Learning

Raspberry Pi can be integrated into various classroom subjects to make learning more interactive and engaging:

1. Mathematics: Use Raspberry Pi to teach concepts like geometry, algebra, and data visualization by creating projects such as graphing calculators or 3D visualizations.

2. Art and Design: Incorporate Raspberry Pi into creative projects like interactive art or digital signage. Students can use the Pi to control lights, sounds, or visual displays in art installations.

3. History and Geography: Use the Raspberry Pi to create interactive maps or simulations of historical events. Students can use geographic information systems (GIS) or 3D modeling software to explore historical landmarks.

Step 5: Setting Up Raspberry Pi-Based Workshops

For workshops or extracurricular activities, the Raspberry Pi can be used to teach a variety of skills, from basic coding to advanced robotics. Here's how you can set up an effective Raspberry Pi-based workshop:

1. **Plan the Curriculum**:

- o Start with the basics: teaching students to install **Raspberry Pi OS**, use the terminal, and write basic Python programs.
- o Gradually move to more advanced topics like **IoT**, **robotics**, **machine learning**, and **web development**.
- o Offer hands-on projects, such as building weather stations, robots, or simple web apps, to solidify students' learning.

2. **Create Learning Materials**:
   - o Provide step-by-step guides for each project.
   - o Include **example code**, hardware wiring diagrams, and explanations of the concepts involved.
   - o Encourage collaborative learning by allowing students to work in teams and share ideas.

3. **Use Online Resources**:
   - o Utilize online platforms like **Raspberry Pi Foundation**, **GitHub**, and **YouTube** to find tutorials, resources, and project ideas.
   - o Encourage students to explore and contribute to open-source projects.

Final Thoughts

The **Raspberry Pi** is a powerful and affordable educational tool that empowers both students and educators. By integrating the Pi into schools and workshops, you can teach a wide range of subjects, from **programming** and **electronics** to **robotics** and **data science**. Its versatility and the vast number of available resources make it an ideal platform for hands-on, project-based learning.

In this chapter, we explored how to use the Raspberry Pi for **interactive science experiments** and teaching **programming**, along with robotics and other exciting educational projects. With the Raspberry Pi, the possibilities are endless, and it's a fantastic way to inspire the next generation of innovators, makers, and engineers.

CHAPTER 26

TROUBLESHOOTING AND MAINTENANCE

Common Troubleshooting Tips and How to Maintain Your Raspberry Pi

The **Raspberry Pi** is a reliable and versatile platform, but like any piece of technology, it can occasionally encounter issues. Whether you're using your Raspberry Pi for simple projects or advanced applications, knowing how to troubleshoot and maintain it is essential to ensure smooth operation and long-term reliability.

In this chapter, we'll explore common troubleshooting tips and maintenance strategies for the Raspberry Pi, as well as how to ensure the long-term reliability of your projects.

Step 1: Common Troubleshooting Tips

1. Raspberry Pi Not Booting Up

If your Raspberry Pi isn't booting up properly, here are some steps you can take to diagnose and resolve the issue:

- **Check the Power Supply**: Ensure that your Raspberry Pi is receiving adequate power. A low-quality or underpowered **micro-USB** or **USB-C** power supply can cause booting issues. Make sure you're using a **5V 2.5A** power supply (for Raspberry Pi 3) or a **5V 3A** power supply (for Raspberry Pi 4).
- **Check the SD Card**:
  - Ensure the **microSD card** is inserted properly into the Raspberry Pi. If it's not fully inserted, the Pi won't boot.
  - Try using a different **microSD card** with a fresh installation of **Raspberry Pi OS**. Sometimes, corrupted SD cards can cause boot problems.
- **Check the LED Indicators**:
  - The **green LED** on the Raspberry Pi should blink when it's reading from the SD card. If it stays off or is solid, there may be an issue with the SD card or OS installation.
  - The **red LED** should stay solid if there's power, but it may blink or turn off if there's a power issue.

- **Reinstall Raspberry Pi OS**: If your Raspberry Pi still isn't booting, try reformatting your microSD card and reinstalling **Raspberry Pi OS** from scratch using the **Raspberry Pi Imager**.

2. No Display on the Screen

If you see a black screen on your monitor, it could be due to several issues:

- **Check the HDMI Cable and Monitor**: Make sure the HDMI cable is securely connected and that the monitor is set to the correct input source. Try using a different cable or monitor if needed.
- **Check the Resolution Settings**:
  - Some monitors may not support the Raspberry Pi's default resolution. If your Pi is not displaying anything, try forcing a specific resolution in the **config.txt** file.
  - To do this, open the **config.txt** file on the microSD card (located at `/boot/config.txt`) and add or uncomment these lines to set the HDMI resolution:

```ini
hdmi_safe=1
```

256

- This setting will automatically configure the Raspberry Pi to work with most monitors.

3. USB Ports Not Working

If your **USB devices** (keyboard, mouse, or external storage) are not working, consider the following:

- **Power Supply Issues**: If the Raspberry Pi isn't receiving enough power, the USB ports may not function properly. Ensure your power supply is sufficient, especially if you're connecting multiple USB devices.
- **Check the USB Connections**: Ensure that the USB devices are properly connected to the Pi. Try using a different USB port or a powered USB hub if you are using power-hungry devices.
- **Check the System Logs**: If a device isn't recognized, check the **system logs** for error messages related to USB devices. Use the following command to view the logs:

```bash
dmesg | grep -i usb
```

4. Network Connection Issues

If you're having trouble with **Wi-Fi** or **Ethernet** connectivity, here are some steps to try:

- **Check Wi-Fi Settings**: Ensure your Wi-Fi credentials are correct. You can configure Wi-Fi via the desktop interface or by editing the **wpa_supplicant.conf** file on the microSD card.
- **Check IP Address**: If using Ethernet, ensure your Raspberry Pi has an IP address. You can check it by running:

```bash

ifconfig
```

- **Test Connectivity**: Use the `ping` command to test network connectivity:

```bash

ping google.com
```

- **Check Router and Network**: If your Raspberry Pi can't connect to the internet, verify that the **router** is working correctly and that other devices can connect to the same network.

Step 2: Maintaining Your Raspberry Pi

Proper maintenance can help ensure the long-term reliability of your Raspberry Pi and its projects.

1. Keep the Raspberry Pi Clean

Raspberry Pi devices can get quite dusty over time, which can cause overheating or hardware malfunctions.

- **Clean the Case and Ports**: Use a soft brush or compressed air to remove dust from the case and ports. Be careful not to let moisture from compressed air get inside the Raspberry Pi.
- **Keep the Cooling System Clean**: If your Raspberry Pi has a **fan** or **heat sink** for cooling, ensure that they are clean and functioning properly to prevent overheating.

2. Back Up Your Projects and Data

Regular backups are essential to prevent data loss in case of system failures.

- **Backup your SD Card**: Use tools like **Win32DiskImager** (Windows) or **dd** (Linux/macOS) to create an image of your **SD card**. This will allow you to restore your system if it becomes corrupted or if you need to reinstall your OS.
- **Cloud Backups**: For projects involving data collection, consider storing critical data in **cloud storage** (e.g., **Google Drive**, **Dropbox**, or **AWS**). This ensures you won't lose valuable information if your Raspberry Pi experiences a failure.

3. Monitor System Performance

To keep your Raspberry Pi running smoothly, it's helpful to monitor its system performance, such as CPU usage, memory, and temperature.

- **CPU Usage**: Use the `top` or `htop` command to monitor CPU usage:

```
bash
```

```
top
```

- **Memory Usage**: Check memory usage using the `free` command:

```
bash
```

```
free -h
```

- **Temperature**: Overheating can lead to system instability. You can check the temperature of your Raspberry Pi using:

```
bash
```

```
vcgencmd measure_temp
```

- **System Logs**: Keep an eye on system logs for errors or warnings. The logs can be found in `/var/log/` and can be viewed with commands like:

```
bash
```

```
cat /var/log/syslog
```

4. Update Software Regularly

Regularly updating the software on your Raspberry Pi ensures that you have the latest features, security patches, and bug fixes.

- **Update the OS**: Run the following commands to update **Raspberry Pi OS**:

```bash
sudo apt-get update
sudo apt-get upgrade
sudo apt-get dist-upgrade
```

- **Update Installed Software**: Make sure that all installed packages, including libraries and applications, are up to date.

Step 3: Ensuring Long-Term Reliability for Your Projects

To ensure the longevity and reliability of your Raspberry Pi projects, it's important to consider a few best practices:

1. Use Proper Cooling and Ventilation

Raspberry Pi can overheat during long-running tasks. This is especially true if you're using it for CPU-intensive tasks, such as **AI processing**, **gaming**, or **multimedia applications**.

- **Active Cooling**: Use a **fan** or **heat sinks** to dissipate heat more effectively.
- **Enclosure with Ventilation**: If you are using the Raspberry Pi in an enclosure, ensure that it has proper ventilation or openings for airflow.

2. Use a UPS (Uninterruptible Power Supply)

Power interruptions can damage your Raspberry Pi and lead to data corruption. To protect against power failures, consider using a **UPS** to ensure that the Raspberry Pi has consistent power.

3. Use Quality SD Cards

SD cards are often the most common point of failure in Raspberry Pi projects, especially when they are constantly written to. Always use high-quality, reliable SD cards (preferably **Class 10** or **UHS-1** cards) to avoid corruption and failures.

263

4. Design Redundancy and Failover Systems

For critical applications, consider building **redundant systems** or **failover mechanisms**. For example:

- **Automated backups**: Set up scheduled backups to a secondary storage device or cloud service.
- **Multiple Pis**: In high-availability projects, use multiple Raspberry Pis with **load balancing** or **failover mechanisms** to ensure the system remains operational in case one Raspberry Pi fails.

Final Thoughts

The **Raspberry Pi** is a powerful and versatile tool for both hobbyists and professionals, but like any piece of technology, it requires proper maintenance and troubleshooting to ensure long-term reliability. In this chapter, we covered common troubleshooting tips, maintenance practices, and strategies to keep your Raspberry Pi and its projects running smoothly.

By regularly maintaining your Raspberry Pi, backing up your data, monitoring system performance, and ensuring proper cooling and power supply, you can extend the life of your Raspberry Pi and enjoy seamless performance for years to come.

CHAPTER 27

FUTURE OF RASPBERRY PI PROJECTS

New and Upcoming Raspberry Pi Models and Their Features

The **Raspberry Pi** has come a long way since its inception in 2012, evolving into a powerful and versatile platform for makers, educators, and hobbyists alike. As of now, Raspberry Pi models continue to improve, offering more features, enhanced performance, and greater flexibility for a variety of projects.

In this chapter, we'll explore the **future of Raspberry Pi projects**, focusing on the **new and upcoming Raspberry Pi models**, their features, and how you can stay ahead of the curve by utilizing these advancements in your own projects. We'll also discuss ways to keep up with emerging technology to ensure you continue building innovative projects with the Raspberry Pi.

Step 1: New and Upcoming Raspberry Pi Models

266

The Raspberry Pi Foundation consistently releases new models and upgrades to meet the growing demand for more powerful, energy-efficient, and versatile computing solutions. Here are some of the most recent and upcoming models that are shaping the future of Raspberry Pi projects:

1. Raspberry Pi 4 Model B

The **Raspberry Pi 4** is the most powerful model in the Pi lineup, offering substantial upgrades over previous versions in terms of processing power, memory, and connectivity.

- **Key Features**:
    o **Quad-core Cortex-A72 processor** running at **1.5 GHz** (a significant speed improvement over the Raspberry Pi 3).
    o **Up to 8GB RAM** (previous models had 1GB, 2GB, or 4GB options), allowing for better multitasking and more complex applications.
    o **Two 4K HDMI outputs**, supporting dual monitors for more versatile use cases like media centers and workstations.
    o **USB 3.0 ports** for faster data transfer speeds.
    o **Gigabit Ethernet** for better network connectivity.

- o **Dual-band Wi-Fi** (2.4GHz and 5GHz) and **Bluetooth 5.0** for faster and more reliable wireless connections.
- o **Power over Ethernet (PoE)** support (with an additional HAT) for easier power management in industrial or outdoor setups.

- **Use Cases**:
  - o **Media centers** (using **LibreELEC** or **OSMC**).
  - o **Robotics** and **AI applications** (leveraging the increased memory and processing power).
  - o **Home automation** with expanded connectivity.
  - o **Multitasking and desktop computing**.

The **Raspberry Pi 4** offers the most robust hardware, making it suitable for advanced projects, from **IoT** to **AI**.

2. Raspberry Pi Zero 2 W

The **Raspberry Pi Zero 2 W** is an exciting addition to the Pi lineup, combining the small form factor of the original **Pi Zero** with improved performance.

- **Key Features**:
  - o **Quad-core Cortex-A53 processor** running at **1 GHz** (four times faster than the original Pi Zero).
  - o **512MB RAM**, which is more than sufficient for most lightweight projects.

268

- o **Wireless LAN** (Wi-Fi) and **Bluetooth 4.2** for easy connectivity in remote projects.
- o **Small form factor**, ideal for compact, portable applications.
- o **GPIO pins** for hardware interfacing.

- **Use Cases**:
  - o **Wearables** and **portable projects** (due to its small size).
  - o **Embedded systems** in IoT projects.
  - o **Retro gaming consoles** (running lightweight emulators like RetroPie).
  - o **Remote sensors** and **data logging**.

The **Zero 2 W** is an excellent option for projects requiring a small footprint with decent processing power at an affordable price.

3. Raspberry Pi Pico and RP2040 Chip

The **Raspberry Pi Pico** is the first **microcontroller** from the Raspberry Pi Foundation, based on the **RP2040 chip**. Unlike previous Raspberry Pi models, which are single-board computers, the Pico is designed for embedded applications that require low-level control over hardware.

- **Key Features**:

- o **RP2040 microcontroller** with a **dual-core ARM Cortex-M0+ processor** running at 133 MHz.
- o **264KB RAM** and **2MB flash memory** (for storing programs).
- o **GPIO pins** for hardware interfacing.
- o **Support for Python (MicroPython) and C** for development.
- o **Low power consumption**, ideal for battery-operated projects.

- **Use Cases**:
  - o **Embedded systems** (such as sensors, actuators, and automation).
  - o **DIY electronics** projects like robotics, home automation, and wearables.
  - o **IoT devices** with wireless communication (using additional modules like **Wi-Fi** or **Bluetooth**).

The **Pico** and **RP2040** chip offer exciting possibilities for smaller, more power-efficient projects where you need fine control over hardware and don't require a full operating system.

4. Upcoming Models: Raspberry Pi 5 and Beyond

While the **Raspberry Pi 5** has not yet been released, the Raspberry Pi Foundation is always working on improvements. Expectations for future releases include:

- **Faster processors** and improved **graphics capabilities** for more demanding tasks like **gaming** and **AI processing**.
- **More RAM options** (possibly up to **16GB**), which will make the Raspberry Pi even more suitable for **server** or **workstation** applications.
- **Better AI and ML support**, with hardware acceleration for deep learning models.

Step 2: How to Keep Up with Emerging Technology and Continue Building Innovative Projects

The Raspberry Pi ecosystem is constantly evolving, and as new models, software updates, and peripherals are released, it's essential to keep up with emerging technology. Here's how you can stay ahead of the curve:

1. Participate in the Raspberry Pi Community

The **Raspberry Pi community** is one of the most active and engaged communities in the world. By participating, you can stay informed about the latest developments and share your own projects with others.

- **Raspberry Pi Forums**: The official Raspberry Pi Forums are a great place to discuss issues, find solutions, and share ideas with other Pi enthusiasts.
- **Reddit and Social Media**: Subreddits like **r/raspberrypi** and **r/raspberrypiprojects** are excellent places to discover new projects, tutorials, and ask questions.
- **GitHub**: Many open-source projects are available on GitHub. You can contribute to ongoing projects or start your own.

2. Follow Official Raspberry Pi News

The Raspberry Pi Foundation regularly updates its official blog and social media channels with the latest news about upcoming models, software updates, and official releases. These platforms also provide educational content, tutorials, and projects.

- **Raspberry Pi Blog**: Follow the official blog for announcements and tutorials.

- **Raspberry Pi Newsletters**: Subscribe to their newsletters to get updates directly in your inbox.

3. Experiment with New Hardware and Peripherals

As new **Raspberry Pi accessories** and **add-ons** (such as camera modules, sensors, displays, etc.) are released, experiment with these in your projects to expand your skills and capabilities.

- **Raspberry Pi HATs**: These are hardware add-ons that can provide additional functionality (e.g., motor control, sensors, or additional I/O ports).
- **Third-party peripherals**: Many manufacturers create additional accessories for the Raspberry Pi, such as **touchscreens**, **robotic kits**, and **audio interfaces**.

4. Learn New Programming Languages and Frameworks

The Raspberry Pi supports a wide range of programming languages and frameworks. By learning new programming skills, you can stay adaptable and capable of tackling a variety of projects. For example:

- **Python**: The primary language for Raspberry Pi projects, especially in **IoT** and **AI** applications.

- **C/C++**: For low-level control and performance-critical applications.
- **JavaScript/Node.js**: For web-based applications and **IoT** integrations.
- **Machine Learning Libraries**: Experiment with **TensorFlow Lite** and **OpenCV** for AI and computer vision projects.

5. Experiment with Cloud Integration

As IoT and cloud computing continue to grow, integrating your Raspberry Pi projects with cloud services is an important trend. You can use cloud platforms like **AWS IoT**, **Google Cloud**, and **Microsoft Azure** to:

- Store and process data collected by sensors.
- Trigger actions in your Raspberry Pi from remote locations.
- Build scalable, cloud-connected applications.

Final Thoughts

The future of **Raspberry Pi projects** is bright, with new models, enhanced features, and improved capabilities on the horizon. The **Raspberry Pi 4**, **Zero 2 W**, **Pico**, and future models will continue to expand the potential for projects in **IoT**, **AI**, **robotics**, and **education**.

By staying connected with the **Raspberry Pi community**, following the latest trends in **hardware** and **software**, and continuing to experiment with new technologies, you'll be able to build innovative and exciting projects for years to come. Whether you're a hobbyist, educator, or professional, the Raspberry Pi offers endless opportunities to explore and create.

www.ingramcontent.com/pod-product-compliance
Lightning Source LLC
Chambersburg PA
CBHW070939050326
40689CB00014B/3266